It's Hard. But It's Fair

by Charles M. Choice

The contents of this work, including, but not limited to, the accuracy of events, people, and places depicted; opinions expressed; permission to use previously published materials included; and any advice given or actions advocated are solely the responsibility of the author, who assumes all liability for said work and indemnifies the publisher against any claims stemming from publication of the work.

All Rights Reserved
Copyright © 2019 by Charles M. Choice

No part of this book may be reproduced or transmitted, downloaded, distributed, reverse engineered, or stored in or introduced into any information storage and retrieval system, in any form or by any means, including photocopying and recording, whether electronic or mechanical, now known or hereinafter invented without permission in writing from the publisher.

Dorrance Publishing Co
585 Alpha Drive
Suite 103
Pittsburgh, PA 15238
Visit our website at www.dorrancebookstore.com

ISBN: 978-1-4809-5464-9
eISBN: 978-1-4809-5439-7

It's Hard. But It's Fair

Michael Choice "Living the Dream"

Table of Contents

Acknowledgements ix
Foreword xi
Introduction xv

Chapter 1: The Early days 1
White Sox, Arlington, Texas
East Fort Worth Pony Baseball League, Fort Worth, Texas
Mansfield Youth Athletic Association, Mansfield, Texas
Pirates Baseball Team

Chapter 2: Kansas City Monarchs Select Baseball Team 11
Sundowner Select Baseball League at MLK Park, Fort Worth, Texas
Diversity is power
2002 USSSA 12 & Under World Series, Hutchinson, Kan.

Chapter 3: Playing for Recreational Youth Teams verses Select
Baseball Teams 19

Chapter 4: Youth Baseball Is Huge In Texas 23
Select Baseball Inc., Mesquite, Texas
Cow Town Park Burleson, Texas
Boys Baseball Inc. Mesquite, Texas
Arc Park, Fort Worth, Texas

Chisel Park Mesquite, Texas

Chapter 5: The Great Impasse 27
Image Select Baseball Team, 15's
2005 AAU 16 & Under National Tournament N.O., La.
Dallas Panther Select Baseball Team 15's

Chapter 6: The Home Stretch Playing Select Baseball 31
Dallas Giants Select Baseball Team 16's
Dallas Mustangs Select Baseball Team 18's

Chapter 7: Mansfield Timberview High School 35
Head Coach Robert Owens
Correct decision to drop playing varsity basketball

Chapter 8: The Choice Family Proactive Approach 41
Michael's selection, 25 college baseball programs to contact
Our trip together to Atlanta Perfect Game top S.E. Prospect event

Chapter 9: The University of Texas at Arlington, Arlington, Texas 45
Head Coach Darin Thomas
2009 USA Baseball Collegiate National Team
Three unforgettable seasons
The final year, full of distractions

Chapter 10 Michael Choice Through the Eyes Of Scott Lacefield 63
Some tidbits from behind the scene, Scott recalls from Michael's
College career that he shares in his writings.

Chapter 11: Our Advisors Jeff Frye & Jim Schwanke 97
Parents need the best advice to avoid breaking NCAA rules
& how to deal with MLB scouts and the gray areas about the draft

Chapter 12: 2010 MLB First Year Players Draft -June 7, 2010 101
The happiest baseball day for Michael and the Choice family

Chapter 13: Oakland Athletics Baseball Club 107
Area Scout Armann Brown
July 29, 2010, Michael receives $2 million signing bonus
Vancouver Canadians Short-Season Class A
Kane County Cougars Playoffs Chicago, Ill

Chapter 14: 2011 Oakland Athletics Spring Training. 111
Non-Roster Invitee

Chapter 15: 2011 Stockton Ports. 115
Oakland Athletics Hi-A Affiliate
Arizona Fall League Rising Stars Game

Chapter 16: 2012 Midland RockHounds. 119
Oakland Athletics AA Affiliate

Chapter 17: 2013 Sacramento River Cats 121
Oakland Athletics AAA Affiliate

Chapter 18: 2013 Oakland Athletics Baseball Club. 123

Chapter 19: 2014 Texas Rangers Baseball Club. 125

Chapter 20: In Conclusion. 129

Acknowledgements

I want to give a special thanks to Scott Lacefield for the contributions he made to this book. Scott edited my writings and added significant details and data about Michael's collegiate baseball career from his perspective while they were at the University of Texas Arlington. Scott was the Sports Information Director and Media Guide at UTA. He mentored Michael on how to be most effective giving interviews. He shared in this book significant behind the scene moments of Michael the baseball player and person in Chapter 10, "Michael Choice Through the Eyes of Scott Lacefield." I have the utmost respect for Scott's work ethic and his professional approach given to this project.

I also would like to thank the following coaches who played a significant role in Michael's growth as a baseball player and person.

- Coach Denny Dixon, The Image Baseball Club
- Coach Sam Carpenter, The Dallas Mustangs Baseball 18's
- Coach Robert Owens, Mansfield Timberview High School
- Coach Darin Thomas, University of Texas Arlington
- Coach K.J. Hendricks, University of Texas Arlington
- Coach Jay Sirianni, University of Texas Arlington

There were others who also contributed to Michael's growth as a baseball player and are too many to mention. You know who you are, and we thank you for all you have done for Michael.

Foreword

Baseball is known as "the great American past time." For many African Americans, that is not true. Perhaps because it is often slow-moving, lacking non-stop excitement, and pizzas, like basketball and football, causing an alarming number of African American parents to discourage their children from playing baseball. That was not the case for me. I grew up in Ohio where nearly every young boy was introduced to baseball at an early age. I was no exception as I participated in Little League, Babe Ruth League, American Legion League, and high school baseball. While attending college in Georgia, I played baseball for two years. Because of the need to complete an academic requirement for graduation, I could not play baseball my senior year. I was fulfilling my mandatory business internship with Union Oil of California and could not get off early enough to make the 4 P.M. practice time. I went to the head baseball coach's home, asking for his permission, allowing me to be 30 minutes late for practice. He would not make an exception, therefore my baseball career ended abruptly. I was an outstanding collegiate catcher with dreams of playing professionally. I was consumed with bitterness because my big-league dreams ended as they did. It was my mother, who challenged me one day by saying, "You can continue being bitter the rest of your life because of a lost opportunity to play professional baseball, or be grateful you earned a college degree through an athletic scholarship." I remember that day vividly and my mother's words of wisdom. I changed my outlook on life and concentrated on my business career by setting attainable goals. Nineteen years later on November 10, 1989, things changed significantly when the Lord blessed me and my wife Charea with our son Michael. The following spring, I began watching professional baseball games on TV once again with a renewed interest, hoping deep within my son would one day show an interest in the game I love so much.

This is a story about my son, Michael Blair Choice, who was introduced to baseball at the age of four. His baseball journey is heartwarming in so many ways. After reading this book, I am hoping you will conclude that, in America, anything is possible. Michael fell in love with baseball right away and made our job as parents easy. We supported him in every way possible. Although playing youth baseball proved to be very expensive as the years went by, we sacrificed in numerous ways to allow his dream to continue. That included juggling finances to buy equipment, afford league and tournament fees, instruction fees, and traveling expenses. All of our vacations were centered around baseball. As good parents should, we were happy to support our son and would do it all over again.

We never forced baseball on Michael. He showed athleticism and good hand-eye coordination when he was young, as early as when he started walking. We bought him a large plastic bat and ball that he played with all the time. It was humorous to watch him drag his bat all over the house. He could hit that ball so hard you had to always be alert or pay a stinging price after the ball bounced off your head. Perhaps we were motivated by his enthusiasm, so we pursued all the available opportunities for him to play baseball in the Dallas/Fort Worth Metroplex area. It was very apparent that African American participation was very low as we visited the many baseball parks in the area. I really wasn't too sure why. Yet as the years went by, it became clear that there were multiple reasons. I will point those reasons out in the following chapters.

Baseball is the ultimate team sport, mirroring life in many ways. The many lessons learned can mold a young child into becoming a better person. To progress to the various levels of expertise requires many years of practice, multiple drills, top-level competition, tremendous athletic ability, solid coaching, and good physical and mental health. Most of the young kids growing up playing baseball will tell you, their ultimate goal is to make it to the Major Leagues. The harsh reality is that most won't make it that far. By sharing my son's story, I will point out some of the many lessons our family learned that could be valuable to parents who have children playing baseball today, who are serious about the game, and show long-range project ability.

It's Hard. But It's Fair

Michael Choice has always played baseball at a high-skill level as he progressed through the early years of the baseball ranks. Yet after an outstanding high school career, he was overlooked and under the radar by college recruiters and Major League Baseball scouts as well. This was even after posting a .506 batting average by season end, ranking sixth overall in the entire DFW area as a high school senior. Michael received one NCAA D-I baseball scholarship offer from The University of Texas at Arlington three weeks before graduating from Mansfield Timberview. He also went undrafted in the MLB Draft in 2007. As a family, we were not disappointed because Michael was only 17-years-old. Going to college was in his best interest. He became draft eligible after completing three years of college. Michael took advantage of that one baseball scholarship offer and had a stellar career at UT Arlington. And oh, how things changed! If you were to ask almost anyone back in June 2007 to predict Michael's baseball future, there would only be a few people that would project what would become reality for Michael. Every year, Major League Baseball has its First-Year Players Draft, where 1,500 baseball players are selected in 50 rounds. These are considered the best prep and collegiate eligible players in the country. On June 7, 2010, Michael Choice was the 10th player selected in the first round by the Oakland Athletics. On July 29, 2010, he signed a professional minor league contract, which included a $2,000,000.00 signing bonus.

Introduction

The chapters to follow will start with Michael's initial baseball experience playing as a 4-year-old for the White Sox, coached by Curt, where they used orange traffic cones for bases. The kids wore shorts, White Sox jerseys, and ball caps. It was simply a group of little boys and girls being exposed to playing together while forming a team. Michael loved it so much, we signed him up for the second two-week session.

Michael's first competitive baseball experience was playing in the East Fort Worth Pony Baseball League. The age groups included Tee Ball (6-year-olds-Twins), Coach Pitch (7-8-year-olds-Dodgers and Giants) and 9-year-old Kid Pitch-Pirates.

This chapter will provide the first glimpse of Michael's gifted athletic ability. When players compete, it is clear which players stand out. Every league has multiple rules that are enforced by a hand full of selected adults. Most of these adults are fair. Some are consumed with the power they have over parents, coaches, and players. Michael played for the Twins when he was 6-years-old. I volunteered to be the Team Dad. The next year, I started coaching Michael. We were the Dodgers. I decided to coach simply because it was clear far too many volunteer coaches did not understand the game, and it was clearly in my son's best interest to get the best baseball coaching that was available. Sometimes fathers who coached their sons for the same reason. Yet there were other fathers who used the coach's title to put their kid above competition. The term "Daddy Ball" defines those coaches. Michael was always one of the better players on my teams. He started because of his ability on the field, not because I was the coach. I coached Michael for six years. If I had continued coaching my son, it may have caused him to get burned out. Dads have a tendency to be too hard on their sons pushing them too hard.

All the youth leagues and teams are discussed in the following chapters. I share many of Michael's noteworthy accomplishments. Each level of competition provided an accumulation of valuable skills needed that all players must master. Baseball is a sport that requires many long hours of practices and competition for players to achieve greatness. There are no short cuts. Most players start playing at a young age to increase their chances to play college and professional baseball.

I will try to break down youth baseball and develop an understanding of the various levels of play. You, as the parent, should determine what is the best for your child. Unless you have an abundance of money to spend. I'll describe the route we went with Michael to continue improving his skills. I learned that there are always people around youth baseball willing to take your money to offer hitting, pitching, and catching lessons. Don't get me wrong, most have best intentions, but often it is all about those offering lessons to earn an honest income. Perhaps your child could take lessons year-after-year and never hit on the level good enough to succeed in baseball. When Michael turned 13, someone other than me coached him. Some coaches were good, others were horrible! It was hit or miss. We decided that every summer would stand on its own. At the end of a season, we would evaluate and then make plans for the following year. I was always there to support Michael and to smooth out any wrinkles. Once Michael turned 15-year-old, we tried to be as accurate as we could, deciding on the best select-baseball team for Michael. I'll devote a chapter to discuss the good, bad, and the ugly. The different personalities often created obstacles to get around ensuring Michael played in the most competitive environment. It was clear to me Michael would need this to play high school, hopefully college, and above.

When Michael was 17-years-old, he tried out for the Dallas Mustangs, an 18-year old select-baseball team coached by Sam Carpenter. I remember it like it was yesterday. It was December 2006, over 100 players were trying out for the few openings available. Michael made that team and gave him the opportunity to play for a nationally known youth coach, who coached multiple players who have played in Major League Baseball. I provide a chapter to this experience and how it helped Michael play on such an outstanding level in college.

My goal is to provide the most accurate description of how Michael was able to progress at a timely pace by working hard, paying attention to detail, having a self-start initiative, and above all, playing for a well-coached team with a very competitive schedule.

I'll devote a chapter for Michael playing for UT Arlington. It was a storybook experience for our family. To this day, Michael's experience at UTA has me shaking my head in awe. Those three years flew by, and only now do I find myself reliving certain games. When Michael was invited to try out for the USA National Collegiate Team, we were so happy for him to get that opportunity. Just as I had my speech prepared to say, "Don't be down on yourself for not making the team," I get a call from Michael at the USA Baseball training facility saying, "Dad, I was selected. I made the team." I was speechless and teary eyed! I will share his experiences with Team USA playing games from North Carolina, Boston Red Sox Fenway Park, Japan, and British Columbia.

I will detail just how wild a ride Michael's last year at UT Arlington was. Words will not describe that nerve-racking experience of every day. Every day was filled with many distractions, as the MLB Draft was to take place in June. Michael had played himself into a position where he was being projected as a first-round pick. But at the same time, he was focused on playing on the field, seemingly ignoring the numerous scouts at every game.

Finally, I will share draft day and what transpired. I'll take you behind the scenes giving you the full scoop. It was an unbelievable day! An absolute dream comes true for Michael. I know firsthand that the Michael Choice baseball story is a good one because he is like many baseball players in America who start out playing tee ball with hopes of playing professional baseball. I'm Michael's dad, saying to you that through hard work, paying attention to detail, along with good health, your child can accomplish the same goal!

Chapter 1
The Early Days

When Michael was 4-years-old, he was the All-American boy: rough, tough, and full of energy. He loved playing outside. We erected a swing and slide set in the back yard that he enjoyed every day. His favorite toys were any of the balls we bought him. His eye-hand coordination was clearly exceptional. He could catch and throw a soft baseball five to seven feet with ease. We took note and found a small glove and a plastic bat and ball.

I'd play with him in the back yard often. It was amazing how hard he could hit the baseball. I used an underhand toss and quickly learned to protect my face because if not, I would surely pay a painful price.

In early September, my wife Charea noticed an advertisement from the Arlington Recreation Center offering an Introduction to Baseball Camp for 5-year-olds. We wasted no time enrolling Michael. There were enough kids registered to form four teams. Michael was assigned to the White Sox team, coached by Curt. The camp ran for two weeks, going two hours every evening. Fundamental baseball skills were taught. Having fun was the most important thing. Boys and girls participated and were cute little smurfs that were hilarious to watch going through the drills. Each kid received a team hat and jersey that they wore proudly. Most kids were simply having fun. We observed Michael paying attention to everything Curt was teaching and later, executing flawlessly. They used orange traffic cones for bases. Most kids found it difficult to understand how to run bases in the correct order. A small hitting tee was used. A soft baseball was placed on top of the tee. Each kid would attempt to hit the ball off the tee and then run the bases. You never knew which base the kids would run to first if they made contact with the ball. Most would swing and miss while trying to make contact with the ball. How very humorous it was for the parents to sit in their lounge chairs laughing at their kids having fun. Michael was having fun, but was very serious about hitting off the tee and running the bases. He was the only child I can recall that was hitting the ball off the tee into the outfield. When we would get home from the two-hour sessions, he wanted to continue practicing in the backyard. Before enrolling in the camp, Michael and I often played catch and soft toss with his plastic bat and ball in the back yard. It was because of those many backyard sessions that Michael was way ahead of the other kids at the camp.

Michael enjoyed the baseball camp so much, we decided to sign him up for the second two-week session. With a new group of 5-year-olds, it was just like the first session, where most kids were lacking good eye-hand coordination. Curt would use Michael to demonstrate the various drills to be mastered by the end of the session. Michael relished the opportunity to show what he could do. Many parents would ask me how long he had been practicing. I'd always say the same thing. Michael loved to play catch in the backyard. It was something he and I would always do. When he got older and outgrew the backyard, we would use the street in front of the house to play long toss.

Michael, age six

Over the winter months, I started investigating what youth baseball leagues were in our area. Through a co-worker, I received information about The East Fort Worth Pony Baseball League. It wasn't a long distance from Arlington and seemed to be perfect for Michael. The Shetland Division was for tee ball players age six. We signed Michael up in January to play in the spring of 1996. This league was well organized with playing fields located at the end of a long gravel road. It was picturesque, with each age group 6-14 years of age while fields were aligned back-to-back. Michael was assigned to the Twins. The team started practicing in March with both boys and girls on the team. Michael and one other player were the only players who could catch and throw. The two of them accounted for most of the put outs, and they had a great time that spring. In tee ball, everyone on the team got to hit. Michael hit the ball hard and a long way. The baseball used was a soft spongy-type that would not injure the kids if they got hit. It was extremely difficult to hit the baseball over the outfield fence, yet Michael hit four home runs that spring. It was clear he was ahead of most players his age. Above all, he loved playing baseball, and that was the most important thing. At the conclusion of that season, Michael was selected to play on the All-Star team to represent the league in a few area tournaments. These tournaments prepared teams to compete in the Pony sanction Shetland Tee Ball District Tournament. This was a very competitive run for East Fort Worth. They did very well in all the tournaments, but were defeated in the district tournament. Michael learned a very valuable lesson in one tournament. He threw his bat after hitting the ball off the tee and was disqualified. He was devastated, crying all the way home. The next day, I came to his rescue with the perfect drill. We went to a local baseball park where I placed the batting tee at home plate. I had Michael to hit the ball off the tee and run to first base carrying the bat half way before simply dropping it from his hand. We repeated this process multiple times. That simple drill worked! Michael never threw his bat again.

The next year, I made a very important decision to become a head coach in the league. I recognized by in large there were very few coaches that knew enough about baseball to be effective teaching the young players the fundamentals. Furthermore, I did not want to short-change Michael, who had proven he had the potential to excel while playing the game of baseball. The East Fort Worth Pony Baseball League had a very stringent approval process to become a head coach in their league, which included a background check. After approximately two weeks, I was approved. Then I learned more about what other obligations the league demanded of head coaches: two concessions stand dates from your team during the season, field duty (mowing and lining the infield) twice during the season, and a mandatory $300/team fee.

Now, on the surface, that does not seem like much, but on top of all the other things, head coaches had to endure from some dysfunctional parents and league officials; it proved to be like having daggers in your side! I would coach two seasons at East Fort Worth Pony Baseball League. For the most part, I enjoyed the experience.

Michael, age seven

The first year we were the Dodgers, a 7-year-old coach-pitch team. My assistant coach was Benny. He and I worked well together and his son Benny Jr. was a very good player on our team. Every age group had a player draft held in the spring following registration and a tryout with throwing, fielding, and hitting. Players received a rating by all the coaches, 1-10, based on their performance. At the draft, every coach could select a player by round until every team had selected 12 players. It was perhaps the easiest way to keep parity for all the teams. To my surprise, I learned politics were always a huge part of the draft. You see, some parents used some unusual tactics, such as little Johnny can only play for coach Joe because of logistics of getting little Johnny to practice and games. There were a lot of requests like that. It was a way to keep their kids from playing for a coach the parent did not know or to stock pile talent. I ended up with my son, little Benny, and a few players no one else wanted. One kid was huge and a known bully. After a couple practices, I was able to get inside his head, convincing him his teammates were depending on him, and he bought into that, and I had no problems with him from that point on. Charlie could hit the ball a ton. To add icing on the cake, his mother volunteered to be team mom, which solved all the communication issues. Michael became a catcher, second baseman, and first base. For a coach-pitch team to be successful, you had to have a coach who could pitch effectively to the kids. Coach Benny Woodard was very good. The kids loved him because he threw at the right speed and angle where their swings were always level. Our team was very competitive. Because of the politics mentioned earlier, some teams were able to have as many as five above-average players, giving them an unfair advantage. Because I knew the game, we would out-coach most teams in our league. Michael was a dominant player who could take over a game with his bat. He hit several homeruns during that spring season. One homer was very special to me personally because it was a defining moment. At age seven, he hit a ball straight away centerfield that landed 50 feet beyond the fence, sailing over a semitrailer used to store equipment in the off-season. I heard someone say to another spectator, "Did you see that? Unbelievable!" No one, I mean no one, could believe a 7-year-old could hit a baseball that far. It was the first time I knew Michael was blessed with God given talent. There were many moments like that over the years, but that was the first. The other significant thing I learned about Michael was he was the best teammate he could be. He wasn't a cocky player in any way. He was never an "I" guy, ever. He laid out everything on the field and would give all he had for the team.

I had two girls on our team that year that were very effective. Taijah was the biggest kid on our team with a big stick and played first base most of the time. Raven was blazing fast, who could beat out most ground balls. If she hit the ball, it was an automatic base hit. So, with Michael, Charlie, little Benny, and our heads up aggressive coaching style, we dominated most of the teams in our division. Some of the coaches that had much better overall talent took loses from the Dodgers very hard. Our two girls were very competitive and if they scored a decisive run against one of the stacked teams, it was worth the price of admission to see the distain on the losing head coach's face. We finished in second place from an eight-team field. At the conclusion of the regular season, Michael was selected to play on the East Fort Worth Coach-Pitch All Star Team. He was one of two 7-year-olds selected. The other players were all 8-years-old. This team was coached by the division champion Twins. I respected this coach, and he understood the game and that sat well with me. He knew Michael was an outstanding player and played him in the right positions, and he helped them win some tournament games. Pony tournaments were very competitive, and playing for the East Fort Worth Pony League was a very good decision.

The next year was even better. Every year each team in its division had to choose what MLB team they would represent. We chose the Giants for this year. The season started out with controversy from the beginning. I asked a former head coach in the league, Michael Carr, to be my assistant coach. His son Mikie had played with Michael on the Twins tee ball team. Many of the coach-pitch team coaches became outspoken saying Mikie, all 50 lbs. of him, paired with my son Michael was an unfair advantage. It was a crazy assertion. It all was put to rest when one levelheaded coach made this statement. "Any good player paired with Michael Choice is an unfair advantage." After loud laughter, the draft took place. I selected ten more players that included mischievous identical twins and eight smurfs. Those twins were good little ball players, but were always distracted. Their single parent mom would chastise them during most games to get them focused. It worked most of the time. We practiced hard, and they had no fear. I would gather my team before every game, have them look at their opponent across the field, and ask the same question, "Do you all care anything about that team over there," they would respond with, "No, Coach!" so I would follow with, "Well, go ahead and whip 'em then!" We destroyed the league winning the coach-pitch championship! Our biggest rival was the Braves. They were stacked with talent and their assistant coach was a retired high school coach who was the grandfather to one of the players. We beat them five straight times!

As I pointed out earlier, the politics within the league were always played out from one issue to another. The board of directors would vote on just about anything. Once I won the league championship, honestly, the sore losers tried to hit me below the belt. To be the All-Star head coach for your division, you had to be the head coach of the league champion and fulfill the three requirements mentioned earlier.

Michael, age eight

I had completed all the above. Yet one week after the regular season ended, I received a call from a board member telling me that I did not have full coverage of one concession stand duty. I was outraged! I remember the evening in question, and I arrived before the first game along with my team Mom and two additional parents. We worked the entire evening until the end of the last scheduled game. Because the board had voted to strip me of the opportunity to be the All-Star coach, my team parents were outraged and fought back, demanding the board reconsider its decision. Finally, they offered a way to resolve the issue by assigning another concession stand date. As much as I knew I was wronged, we agreed to it. Parents from other teams volunteered to work with our team that night. We had so much help, the commissioner of the league asked us to relieve some of the parents, claiming it was a fire hazard. I went on to become the All-Star head coach. We named the team the Spartans. We won several invitation tournaments in the DFW area. Michael was a force while leading the team in hitting. He also hit some towering shots over the left, right, and center field fences. Because of all the drama that year, we decided to find another league for Michael to play in the next season. I had worked diligently for East Fort Worth Pony Baseball League for three years. Perhaps because some were jealous of both my son's baseball skills and the coaching skills I applied. Yes, my son participating motivated me, but I really enjoyed helping the kids with little to no baseball skills become good fundamental baseball players and a positive understanding of what it means to be a member of a team.

Michael and I proudly wearing our Spartan All-Star uniforms

The following spring, we decided Michael would play in the Mansfield Youth Athletic Association. Their baseball complex was located just south of Arlington. There was not enough time or openings for me to have my own team. We were open to what options were left. As I started to look at the best available team for Michael, I was approached by the head coach of the Pirates, John Sawyer, who was interested in Michael playing for his team. John also was open for me to be an assistant coach. He had coached his son, Preston, and ten other players for the past three years. Their families were very close, and their kids all went to the same school. The talent level was incredibly good. It was out of the ordinary for them to add a player outside their inner circle. It was a smart move by John, as he knew firsthand how good of an all-around player Michael was. When adding Michael to the team, it became extremely difficult to beat this team. I agreed with one condition. The Pirates would have to add Michael's neighborhood friend, Terrance, who was also African American. I wanted to be sure Michael would have at least one friend on the team. The players and parents welcomed Michael and Terrance. John was a very smart and savvy coach. We got along fine, with the exception to one team rule he had for the players. All players had to practice wearing white tee shirts or white sweatshirts with no visible markings. I understood what he was trying to accomplish, but I did not like the military approach for 9-year-olds. It seemed to take the fun out of playing baseball. Halfway through the season, I decided to challenge that approach, when I went to a local sporting goods store that had a going out of business sale. I bought black with gold trimmed Pirates jerseys for the entire team to wear during practices. The cost was a mere $2.50 a jersey. I handed the jerseys out at the next practice, insisting that the players wear them. John and I talked about it briefly. He was not pleased. I knew that moment Michael would not play for him after that season. From a baseball position, it was a good year for Michael. He played for a multi-talented team for the first time. He learned many finer points of the game, playing defense and pitching. John and I respected one another, and we would become strong competitors in the years to follow. He changed his team name to Stingrays, and we would play against one another many times down the road. John was a family man with a wonderful wife and children. I respected him on and off the field.

Chapter 2
K.C. Monarchs Select Baseball Team

During the off-season, I thought a lot about the lack of participation in baseball by African American youth. I understood some of the reasons for the lack of participation, and I was determined to do everything I could do to try to make a difference in the DFW area. I decided to create a new team by encouraging primarily African American youth to get parents energized about their kids playing baseball. I decided to name the team the Kansas City Monarchs, to pay homage to the old professional Negro Baseball League. I recruited coaches and players from East Fort Worth Pony Baseball League. The second roadblock was to get the families to travel to Mansfield for games and practices. It took nearly four months to get the team in place. With three roster spots open, a co-worker saying he had players to complete the roster if I was willing to integrate approached me. After a hardy laugh, I was more than happy to have three Caucasian players join the team. It was the better of two worlds because diversity would be our theme. After all, how meaningful it was for those three players to learn all about the Kansas City Monarchs legacy! They won more championships than any other Negro league team with players like Satchel Paige, Jackie Robinson, and Cool Papa Bell. That first year, our team proved to be very competitive while finishing third in the 10-year-old age division. Michael continued to play exceptional baseball. He focused on catching and pitching. We had a strong nucleus of five players who would play together for three consecutive years. Michael became a strong leader who would lead by example on the field. During the off-season, I decided to have tryouts to move the team up and become a select team playing the best competition in the area.

We had 6-7 openings on the roster. Through much communication and meeting other youth coaches eager to get more African Americans playing youth baseball, I was able to find some very talented players that I wasn't aware were available. By the spring, we had our new roster shaped. Although the initial group of five, Michael Choice, Michael Carr, Keith Flemming, Quinn Sharp, and Terrance Frasier, were 11-years-old, the seven new players were 12-years-old. Therefore, we were forced to be a 12 and under select team. We joined the Sundowner Select Baseball League. All of our games were played at the then-new Martin Luther King Baseball Complex in Arlington. We were a very talented baseball team that received a lot of press coverage, including the City of Arlington Mayor, Elsie Odum, who attended one of our games wearing a Monarchs baseball cap. The local media was there, and two newspaper articles were written about our team and why the team was created. Out of the blue, I received a call from a gentleman who had read one of the articles about our team. He represented a group of General Motor's employees, wanting to donate financially to our team. They purchased custom made jackets with K.C. Monarchs lettering and red cleats for all players and coaches. How awesome for our team to receive such generosity from total strangers.

The Monarchs could play competitively with the best teams in our age group in the DFW area. We entered multiple invitational tournaments, winning our fair share. People were not used to seeing a team like ours, with the majority of our roster African Americans with three very talented Caucasian players as well. We preached as coaches that diversity was power! The kids believed that and always played with confidence.

One of the most effective tools I utilized while coaching was videotape by Dr. Bragg Stockton. He authored several videos on baseball fundamentals, "skills and drills." These tapes were about hitting, fielding, throwing, catching, and pitching. I found that I could carefully plan my team practices to maximize time management. Dr. Stockton's tapes offered common sense approach to teach young baseball players the fundamentals of the game, making it fun for eager to learn young players. He is deceased, but his skills and drills tapes are available in DVD format at local sporting goods stores. I encourage youth coaches to consider using Dr. Bragg Stockton's easy to use skills and drills training aides. Your young players are guaranteed to become better players.

It's Hard. But It's Fair

Michael, age 10

One of the teams in our division was the Texas Warriors. The first time I saw them, I told our coaches that we were going to beat that team. They were very small and looked to be a younger team than ours. Our first game against them was a total wake up call. Teams like this remind you to never underestimate your opponent. They destroyed us by winning 17-0. They were incredibly fast. They ran the bases aggressively, and they played flawless defensively. They were very well coached and were very, very cocky. They won our division and won a USSSA qualifying tournament to play in the 12 and under World Series in Hutchinson, Kansas. I was asked by their head coach about Michael's availability to travel to Kansas with their team. We were thrilled and honored with the invitation. They added Michael to their tournament roster as their primary catcher. He was the only 11-year-old selected to their tournament team, which was quite an honor for Michael. The Monarchs came up short losing by a run in another USSSA qualifying tournament and did not make it to Hutchinson that season. My wife and I went with the Texas Warriors to watch Michael play in Kansas. He started five of the seven games and helped the Warriors win crucial games. Although the Texas Warriors came up short, I absorbed valuable information. The Cape County Bandits from Missouri won the 2001 USSSA world championship, giving me the blueprint I would use for the next season's Monarchs team. I went back to Texas with a wealth of information, knowing what pieces to add to my Monarch team to be successful.

Because of the high cost to participate in our league, uniforms, equipment, league and tournament fees, we were very creative to take the financial burden away from the parents. We had a team meeting in November where we issued each player's family with a set amount of raffle tickets to sell by the end of January to cover roughly 95 percent of the above costs. I went out in the community to get local businesses to donate televisions, stereo equipment, authentic jerseys, and many more items to raffle away. That worked very well. Also, we would pan handle using our players in full uniforms with five gallon white paint buckets along the major routes to the Ballpark in Arlington leading to Texas Ranger games. We never collected less than $900 as a team. We divided the money by the number of players for hotel and travel expense. Pan handling laws were passed shortly after that year. We received donations just before the new law went into effect. Our creativity enabled single parent homes and lower income families the opportunity for their kids to play at the highest level of baseball for little to no cost. Most select baseball teams in the area required very high fees to play for them. Often those fees could be between $1,500-$3,000 annually per player. That would eliminate most minorities wanting to participate. The Monarch's coaching staff never got paid like coaches on most select baseball teams.

The 2002 season would be my last year coaching. I made a decision that when Michael turned 13, it was the right age for my son to be coached by someone other than me. It was a very delicate situation coaching my son. I tended to be harder on Michael. I pushed too hard sometimes, and my wife would intervene, making me realize enough was enough! Had I continued coaching Michael, there is little doubt he would have quit playing baseball all together. With the addition of five very talented 12-year-old players, we diligently recruited, made our 2002 K.C. Monarchs select baseball team one of the most talented 12-year-old select baseball teams in the DFW area. Justin Biggins and Marc Govea came from the Blue Raider Youth Baseball league, having a reputation of producing many outstanding players. I had seen them play many times since they were 6-years-old. They always played together on the same team. Once we got one player, it was easy to get the other. We always coveted having those two players. Along with Michael and the core nucleus five Monarchs players, we had no weak spots in our lineup. We had the lethal combination of speed, power, pitching, and solid defense. The big challenge we had as coaches was to harness all the explosive energy. Sometimes you can have too much talent where egos (both players and parents) get in the way. Two last minute additions to our 2002 Monarch team were outfielder Harrison Law and third baseman, Justin Unger. They were outstanding players that made our roster the best it could be. We had originally decided to have an eleven-player roster to avoid playing time issues. But late one night, I got a call from Mr. Unger who was looking for a team for his son to play on. Because he was so persistent, I agreed to give Justin a private tryout the next day prior to our team practice. After thirty minutes of hitting ground balls and watching him hit, I was totally impressed! He was like a vacuum cleaner, fielding every hard-hit grounder. He hit line shot after line shot. When the other coaches arrived, I let them know we had a new player, Justin Unger. Remarkably all 12 players got along perfectly. They worked hard on the field and had fun together horsing around after games and practices away from competition. Once the umpire said play ball, it was all business.

Michael led the team in home runs and in most of the offensive statistical categories. He was one of six players who could take a game over. The opposition always had a huge task, picking the poison, not knowing who to pitch around. We ran the bases with a vengeance, taking a page from last year's league champion, Texas Warriors. We had something they did not have. We had unbelievable power hitting 54 home runs as a team.

Our goal for that year was clear. We wanted to win a USSSA World Series qualifier, go to Hutchinson, Kansas, and win the championship. On March 17 of that season, we defeated the Sting Rays, coached by John Sawyer, 12-4. By winning a USSSA World Series qualifier so early in the season was a huge accomplishment and took a lot of pressure off our team. We knew that half of our goal for the year was achieved. We added one of the best pitchers in our league to our tournament team, Drew Johnson, who would be dominant. From

July 21-28, we would fulfill our second goal by winning the 2002 USSSA 12 and under World Series in Hutchinson.

There was a total of 88 teams from 29 states participating in the World Series in Hutchinson. Ironically, the two teams playing for the championship were both predominately African American. The Xtreme were from Georgia, and our team from Texas. This was quite fitting, offering hope that more African American youth were playing youth baseball.

Michael, along with five other Monarch players, made the All-World team in Hutchinson. Justin Unger, the last player added to our roster at the beginning of the season, was voted MVP of the World Series. Our team received a proclamation from the city of Arlington's Mayor, Elsie Odum, that August. What an experience for our team, being honored at City Hall, my last defining moment as the head coach.

Winning the 2002 USSSA World Series was the most incredible experience for the players, coaches, and families. Michael and his teammates saw what it was like to play baseball on a big stage. It was a once in a lifetime experience. There couldn't have been a better way for me to end my coaching career.

2000 KC MONARCHS

Michael age 10, second row third from left

It's Hard. But It's Fair

2001 KC MONARCHS

Michael age 11, first row far right

2002 KC MONARCHS

Michael age 12, second row far left; USSSA 12 and Under World Series Champions Hutchinson, Kansas

Chapter 3
Playing for Recreational Teams Verses Select Baseball Teams

One of the most debatable decisions parents have to make is what level of play is best suited for your child. The two most common levels of play in youth baseball in most regions of the country are playing in recreational leagues or with a select team. My definition of a recreational team is one that has players with little to average baseball skills that have teams put together based on a sign-up basis that league members will form. The main focus for this group of players is to have fun, develop baseball fundamental skills with little pressure to win or be competitive. In contrast, my definition of a select team is where players with above average baseball skills are placed in a try-out setting where each team is trying to put together the best team possible with the most talented players. These teams play strong competitive schedules. Here are some of the considerations that can be used to make that decision.

- Age of player and maturity
- Honest assessment of your child's baseball skill level
- Family economic status
- Family support system
- Long range project ability

I believe it is not necessary to play select baseball before the age of 11. Those who push their kids to play select baseball earlier could cause them to get burned out. The worst situation to witness is where a very talented player quits baseball because of the pressures to succeed. Most recreational leagues are not costly at all. League fees and uniform cost are often all that is required. Select baseball teams are often very expensive. The average team fees could be ranging from $1,500-$3,500 per season, with coaches and tournament fees on top of that. That being said, as parents look at their budget and understand there are teams available to fit your family finances.

I observed many of the select baseball teams in the DFW area. They prided themselves on beating teams to submission. There was a pecking order, but that could change from year to year because players bounced from team to team. It was all about winning. There were some select teams interested in Michael playing for them, and some never showed any interest at all. After Michael turned 13, we were open for him to play select baseball. Yet, the first sign of nonsense, we would pack up and move on. I knew Michael was an outstanding baseball player who could hit for average and power. He had excellent catching skills with solid infield and outfield experience. It would not have made sense to me to allow any coaches to destroy Michael by not treating him fairly. Our approach was to prepare Michael for high school and college baseball. There were labels put on youth baseball players that were usually not accurate. The most common was to define a player as Triple-A or Major. Many people got caught up in that foolish way of thinking. Many of the players I had seen play were thought to be studs. Some of the players that were anointed for stardom never came close. You, the parent, have to be realistic about your son. As you watch your son develop playing baseball in a very competitive environment, you can recall those magical moments. If, on the other hand, you watched your child do their best, but you know in your heart they are not destined for a higher level of competition, that is alright as well. Know that kind of honesty will better serve your son in the long run. You have to stay focused with goals that are attainable. If learning what it is to be a team player is what your kid takes with him in the game of life, be thankful!

As Michael matured, I always welcomed his opinion on what teams he wanted to play for. He would tell me what teams he would not play for. Knowing how he felt made my responsibility as a parent much easier. Our family habitually invited the various head coaches to our home and listened to their sales pitch for Michael to play for their ball club. Every select team head coach in the DFW area had a reputation that was usually passed on from parent to parent. If the coach was identified as a psycho, then shame on you for letting him within ten feet of your child. Most head coaches were level headed, and we respected their baseball philosophy. We were appreciative of their offer. Most of our decisions were spontaneous. It would be a gut feeling that their team was best suited for Michael.

In the DFW area, most recreational leagues were located in each city. So it was advantageous to find teams closer to home. Getting to games and practices on time was always a priority. Select teams have no boundaries. If you are playing for a select team, it is more about their team philosophy than logistics of where they play games or practice. Most select teams in the DFW area had a regular season schedule and tournament schedule. The combination usually meant you were playing a very competitive season.

Michael was very fortunate to have played as a guest player for multiple select teams. There would be last minute calls asking if he was available for tournament play. He usually blended in with players and made that team better. He enjoyed playing in tournament games, excelling with the better competition. We learned early that being flexible was one way to enhance the opportunity to improve. The more games you play, the more chances you have to improve your game. Often people would tell us what an outstanding baseball player Michael was. Most had no clue how much time Michael worked on improving his game. He hit in the local batting cages often. We practiced with soft-toss drills in the back yard using a net several times a week. I had a bucket of practice balls we would take to a local high school while sometimes, using a hitting tee at home plate, we would empty the bucket several times to keep his swing level hitting to all fields.

There is no perfect blueprint to success in baseball. Most decisions you must make as parents must be made using common sense. One thing I know for certain is the more work your child puts in the game, the better chance he will succeed. Your support as a parent should not be taken lightly. After all, if you have been shown by your kid that he loves the game of baseball, there is no telling how far he can go. Listen to other parents, and investigate the various youth baseball programs in your area. Be flexible. If your child has a horrible season playing for a specific team, work diligently to find a better team for the next season. Your child's happiness is worth more than what others think about any recreational or select team. I have known parents that felt some strong sense of loyalty to teams that treated their child less than they deserved year-after-year. Look out for the money-hungry baseball programs that brag about winning, but can't truly tell you one beneficial reason your child should join their team. These teams are easy to identify. One way to tell is if the coaches are only focused on two or three players' development, not the entire roster. That is the easiest sign of a team you need to avoid. Every player on the team's roster is important. Don't whip out your checkbook when it isn't in your child's best interest. No matter who the coaches are or what friends of your child's might be on that team. There are good people involved in youth baseball. Make sure you find them.

Chapter 4
Youth Baseball is Huge in Texas

Most people know football is favored in Texas. Baseball ranks right behind. The weather is usually perfect for baseball ten months out of the year. That allows youth baseball to play spring, summer, and fall league and tournament schedules with a perfect climate. Along with Florida, California, and other states in the south, Texas can develop youth baseball players at the same rate. Select baseball teams benefit more because money-making tournaments are scheduled with no shortage of teams willing to sign up. There are outstanding high school baseball programs in Texas. Most high school head coaches follow select baseball to assess the talent of players destined to enroll at their schools.

In North Texas, there are outstanding venues for youth baseball. There are beautiful manicured fields with covered stands throughout the area. Several venues are privately owned as money-making facilities. There are city-owned fields as well. There is no shortage of quality baseball venues for youth leagues to play competitive schedules. It is a smooth-running machine fueled by large number of teams, organized leagues, locally owned business-minded people who realize the economic gains for everyone associated with youth baseball. With nationally established youth baseball associations like USSSA, Super Series, AAU, Little League, Pony, etc. sponsoring national tournaments annually, it all ties into making youth baseball strong.

Michael had the opportunity to play at the following venues in the DFW area multiple times, both regular season and tournament games: Cow Town Park (Burleson), Boys Baseball Inc. (Mesquite), Arc Park (Fort Worth), Chisel Park (Mesquite), and Martin Luther King Complex (Arlington).

These venues offered the opportunity for Michael to play multiple games over the years to improve his skill level. He always loved playing on the big stage. Here are some of the national tournaments, teams played for and cities Michael played in while growing up.

- 2001 USSSA 12 & under World Series, Hutchinson, Kan.; Texas Warriors
- 2002 USSSA 12 & under World Series, Hutchinson, Kan.; K.C. Monarchs
- 2003 Super Series 13 & under World Series, Aurora, Colo.; K.C. Monarchs
- 2004 Super Series 14 & under World Series, Mesquite, Texas; Dallas Panthers
- 2005 Super Series 16 & under National Tournament, Omaha, Neb.; Image Baseball Club
- 2005 AAU 16 & Under National Championship, New Orleans, La.; Image Baseball Club
- 2006 AAU 16 & Under National Championship, Jupiter, Fla.; Dallas Giants
- 2006 16 & Under Mickey Mantle World Series, McKinney, Texas; Dallas Giants
- 2007 18 & Under Yankee East Cobb Classic, Atlanta, Ga.; Dallas Mustangs

Some of the most important keys to improving baseball skills are playing baseball at the highest level available as often throughout the year as possible. Barring injury, a player cannot take extended time off from competitive play to stay in shape and in tune with the fundamentals of the game that are a must to play at the highest level.

The youth baseball community is built with players, families, and coaches. Specific age groups interact with one another each year. It is building relationships that become almost just as important as playing baseball. Communication is essential between families that can inform parents about openings on specific teams that have opportunities available for players to be picked up for competitive tournaments. This will lead to lasting relationships with other families that have children at the same age as yours.

I want parents to understand that I knew Michael had the potential to become an outstanding baseball player at age seven. When he hit a home run over a semitrailer far beyond the fence in straight away center field was one of those defining moments for me. It was eye opening! Hearing one of the parent's say, "Did you see that? Wow!" That was independent confirmation of what I was feeling. Michael has been doing something special like that at every age level. There were mammoth home runs, multi-hit games, game winning hits, and great defensive plays in games played all over this country.

If you have experienced the same with your child, then take note. Being honest with yourself concerning your son's ability is important. You never want to get carried away with project ability past the immediate future. Playing Division I college baseball is an attainable goal that will take above average baseball skill to accomplish. There are lower levels of college baseball as well, with Division II and III along with NAIA and junior college as options as well. It is also possible for each of those levels to produce professional players as well. When looking at Michael's talents and abilities, we focused on Michael attending an NCAA Division I program. It is best if you, as parents, encourage your child to set realistic goals while playing youth sports. Don't invest an enormous amount of money if it isn't warranted. On the other hand, when you know in your heart your child has what it takes to go far in baseball, then give them all of your support is the right avenue to take.

Chapter 5
The Great Impasse

While your child plays youth baseball, there are always ups and downs. Over the years, our family experienced all of these and some others along the way. I coached Michael for six years. That put a lot of pressure on both of us. I told him from the beginning, when we are on the field, I was his coach. When we are off the field, I was Dad. That worked well for the most part. Michael would be unhappy if during practice darkness fell before his turn to take batting practice. Like most young players, taking batting practice is the best part of practice. Often Michael would hit last because I needed to work with other players that were struggling to hit consistently. He did not like being pushed to the back of the line. It was wrong for me to expect him to understand. During those six years, Michael was the ultimate team player. He gave it all he had in both games and practices. Because of how hard Michael played the game, there were never any problems with other parents thinking I showed favoritism toward my son. I enjoyed working with all the players and hope I played a small part in helping the other players become better baseball players and better people.

The spring of 2005 was the first time Michael was uncertain what team he was going to play for during the summer. Without going through all the heart-breaking details, I'll just say in life, we can be blindsided. We had an agreement in January to play for a team and would find out in April that the head coach's word was not honorable. I was guilty of thinking a six-year baseball relationship with a fellow coach was a reliable friendship. I really believed our friendship was on the highest level. The pain our family endured was tough to bear as a result of his actions. Yet, there we were, searching for a team with a roster opening. Through a very good friend, Thomas Taylor, who called me late one evening to say, "If you all are willing to drive 60 miles one way to McKinney, Texas, I have found a team for Michael and my son, Nico, to play together on named the Image." We agreed to play for the Image that summer, playing two league games each week at Prosper High School on Tuesday and Thursday evenings at 6 P.M. We drove 240 miles every week. We needed to leave Arlington by 4 P.M. to get to the games on time. The traffic was horrible every evening, just horrible. Yet, we never missed a game. Michael would often leave our van and go straight to the field without warming up. The Image was loaded with talent and was one of the best 15 and under select baseball teams in the DFW area. Coach Denny Dixon was an outstanding youth coach. Michael enjoyed playing for him. He was an outstanding teacher who could teach defensive plays and strategy from the pitcher's mound with the entire team facing him, sitting cross-legged for a solid hour. Besides the long drives during the week, the Image played in a lot of invitational tournaments in the area on the weekends. There were always people talking about the Image. "What is the Image?" "Who names a team the Image?" When we started thumping some of the powerhouse select teams in the area, the talk eventually stopped. We had great pitching, stellar defense, and tremendous offensive talent. Michael was on top of his game, providing the team with outstanding all-around play. That summer, Michael and our family had perhaps one of the best baseball experiences ever. Our friendship with the Taylor family, Thomas, Nikki, and Nico, began that summer and continues to this day. Two tournaments we played in that summer will always be memorable events. We went to Omaha, Nebraska to play up in a 16 and under Super Series National Tournament. While there, we also attended the 2005 Men's College World Series. During the youth tournament, Michael was injured sliding into home plate. The pitcher's cleat came up and sliced Michael's throat, requiring six stitches. It was a freak accident as the pitcher was covering home after throwing a wild pitch. It was not a big deal to Michael. After getting stitched and bandaged, Michael told everyone he would play the next day in the championship game. Although the Image lost the game, Michael hit a 385-foot home run over the right centerfield fence. It was one of those Kodak moments watching that fastball leave the park. The Image came close to making a comeback against a very tough older 16 and under team.

Later that summer, the Image traveled to New Orleans to play in the 16 and under AAU National Championship. Because of a family crisis, coach Dixon was unable to travel to New Orleans. That truly hurt the team, not having his savvy and smart coaching style. The team played very well, representing themselves by being extremely competitive. The venues were very nice. Games were played all over the city of New Orleans. Michael hit a huge home run over power lines in deep centerfield. The ball looked like it possibly would land on Interstate 10. Not many 15-year-old players could hit a ball that far. That trip was bitter sweet. Hurricane Katrina would hit New Orleans three weeks after that tournament. Many of the ball fields we played on, three weeks later, were under water. It had rained hard one morning during the tournament, postponing a game at the University of New Orleans. I remember observing water flowing over the levy on Lake Pontchartrain. It was scary to see. My feelings were overwhelming, as I said out loud, "Lord, help everyone if a hurricane ever hit New Orleans." Like most Americans, we were glued to our television watching all the tragedy that was aired following that disaster.

Destiny is one aspect in life that cannot be precisely explained. Michael's baseball journey has evolved from circumstances that no one could predict. I call it fate. His story has seemed to be predestined. When he was younger and we long tossed in front of our house, he would have a huge smile on his face, letting me know how much he loved baseball. His throws were always thrown hard and crisp. He never seemed to get enough. I have observed other kids that let the heat in Texas drive them back into air-conditioned rooms as soon as possible, not wanting to complete a doubleheader. Not Michael. He never complained. One thing he never accepted was losing games. He played hard and always played to win. I remember our first tournament game in New Orleans, losing 2-1 to a very tough team. Michael pitched a gem, striking out 10, yet coming up short. We had a second game to play later that afternoon. We went to Popeye's Chicken in between games. I talked to Michael the entire time about letting that loss go. In his mind, we should have won that game. Shortly after eating, I challenged him to do everything he could to help the Image win the upcoming game. We won that game 8-5. Michael hit a triple off the top of the left field wall with the bases loaded. There were games like that, I remember well, defining what kind of baseball player Michael was. No one has a crystal ball predicting where a serious baseball player will end up in his career. There are always fewer opportunities to reach the top. Nevertheless, you keep supporting your kid to play the game hard, hoping there is a silver lining awaiting him, rewards for the true diligence.

Chapter 6
The Home Stretch Playing Select Baseball

Playing for the Image Baseball Team in 2005 was very rewarding. Unfortunately, head coach Denny Dixon decided he would not continue coaching the following year. This forced the players to move on to new teams the next summer. This was unfortunate because these players were very talented and had excellent team chemistry.

We decided to listen to all suitors. Then make the best decision where to play the following summer. Through Dave Johnson, father of one of my former players, Drew, we were put in contact with the Dallas Giants head coach. We knew about the Dallas Giants and their reputation of being a very good select team. The Giants head coach set up a time to come to our home to talk with us about Michael playing for his team. After that meeting took place, as a family, we decided Michael would play for his team. Most of their players had played together for a long time. Their talent level was very good. All of their players were 16-years-old, playing on their high school's junior varsity team. Michael was also 16, but was a year ahead academically, having started school at the age of four. He was already playing on Mansfield Timberview's varsity baseball team and would be entering his senior year in the fall. Because the Dallas Giants played up in most tournaments, we were comfortable in deciding to play for them. They were the only 16 and under select baseball team we would have considered playing for because of their strong history. Otherwise, it would have been in Michael's best interest to play up on a 17 and under select team considering he would graduate a year earlier than his Dallas Giants teammates.

The Dallas Giants were different from any team Michael had ever played for. Most of their families were from an aristocratic area in North Dallas. The majority of the families lived in Highland Park. For those unfamiliar with Highland Park, I'll make it simple; former President George W. Bush bought a house in Highland Park where he and his wife Laura live since leaving the White House. It is one of the richest communities in North Dallas. Within the Dallas Giants families were five attorneys and one judge. Yet, they were the nicest group of parents we had been around. They welcomed us with friendliness that was genuine in every way. There were parents like ours that came from a middle-class background, and that made us feel more at ease mingling with amongst the other families. It was our understanding that three parents sponsored the team financially for regular season and tournament game fees. Therefore, we were only responsible for travel and lodging at tournaments. All the regular season games were played at Highland Park High School. The surface was a very expensive artificial turf, where games were never rained out. The logistics of getting to North Dallas from Arlington on Tuesday and Thursday evenings were tough, but after driving to McKinney the previous year, it was manageable.

Michael played well that summer overall. He sustained a high ankle sprain the beginning of the summer, sliding into second base during a tournament game. We used multiple rehabilitation treatment plans that did not heal his ankle completely. He wasn't able to run at full speed until the end of the summer. Once again, Michael had a few Kodak moments that summer exposing his power and ability to play at multiple defensive positions. He never missed any games that summer, but was hobbled for a large portion of the schedule. He played through the pain and was able to contribute helping the Giants to a successful summer. The two most eventful tournaments were the 16 and under AAU Junior Olympic tournament in Jupiter, Florida, and the 16 and under Mickey Mantle World Series in McKinney, Texas. Both tournaments were competitive, and the Dallas Giants played very well in both. Before both of these tournaments, the Giants participated in a Baylor University sponsored team baseball camp. The camp was designed very well, giving all the players exposure. Teams were paired up to play three complete games. Michael played extremely well, getting seven hits in 11 at-bats. He played infield, outfield, pitcher, and catcher. Baylor was one of the schools Michael was interested in.

He had hopes that his solid overall play at the camp would catch their attention. Perhaps because the Giants were a 16 and under team, Baylor assumed none of the players would be seniors in high school the following school year.

They say 20-20 hindsight is worth its weight in gold. Had Michael played on a 17 and under select baseball team that summer, he would have been exposed to more collegiate programs than just Baylor. That being said, everything eventually worked out for Michael. Perhaps the real roadblock for Michael was starting school a year early at a private school at the age of four. He tested so high as a 4-year-old; we felt it was in his best interest to start school early. Athletically, once he moved to public school, he would compete with kids a year older. As a sophomore at Timberview High School, Michael was the starting point guard on the varsity basketball team. He wasn't physically as strong as most of the opposition. Mentally he ran the court well, but against tougher competition, I noticed what a difference one year made. On the baseball field, it was totally different. His skill level was always above his age.

In September 2006, Michael was invited to attend the South East Top Prospect Camp by Perfect Game at East Cobb Sports Complex in Marietta, Georgia. It was an opportunity for Michael to be compared with the best baseball players his age from the Southeast. It was advertised that many college recruiters would be present. This was the most memorable trip Michael and I would have as father and son. It was expensive, but important for Michael, considering he had started his senior year of high school. Early baseball recruiting by colleges was just underway. Michael represented himself very well. He primarily played second base in the workouts. He did pitch in one game. His above average ability to hit with wood bats was most impressive. Jason Heyward, an outfielder now with the Atlanta Braves, was also competing at this camp. He and Michael, along with a few other players, stood out. In the final game of the camp, Michael hit a triple off the top of the left field fence on East Cobb Field No. 1. It was eye popping! Eugene Heyward, Jason's dad, approached Michael and I with some very kind words praising Michael's triple off the wall. He was very impressed with Michael's over all play, encouraging us to talk with the Perfect Game officials about getting an invitation to play with Jason's team in Jupiter, Florida in the Wood Bat World Series two weeks later. As flattering as that was, we were not in the financial position to participate. Nevertheless, our trip to Atlanta was a success. We did receive a phone call from Belmont University in Nashville, Tennessee expressing interest in Michael.

The next important time frame was mid-December. The Dallas Mustangs 18's was having a tryout for a few spots on their next summer team. Michael, along with more than 100 high school players, participated. After two hours of fielding and hitting, Mustangs legendary head coach Sam Carpenter talked to Michael and me. He asked, "Is it possible for you all to come back tomorrow? I want to see Michael hit again. I know doughnuts to dollars Michael can hit, but I'd like to see him hit again tomorrow." We agreed to come back. When Michael and I got home from North Dallas, Michael told me, "I'm going to the skill center to hit." An hour later, he returned saying, "I worked on some things." The next day, we returned to North Dallas. I sat behind home plate high in the stands, watching Michael put on a hitting clinic for the Mustangs coaches. The sound of the ball coming off his bat was loud and different as line shots hit from gap-to-gap. I noticed many of the other ball players at the tryout stopping what they were doing to see who was hitting the baseball in the batting cage. At the conclusion of the tryout, Coach Carpenter talked to Michael privately for 30 minutes. Afterwards, he motioned for me to join them. As we stood there together, Coach Carpenter looked at me and said, "I don't know where I am going to play him, but I want Michael on my team." I remember driving home from North Dallas and how excited we both were. Playing for the Dallas Mustangs 18's was an honor for any 17-year-old. Coach Sam Carpenter's reputation in the DFW area was impeccable. We called our good friends in McKinney, Thomas and Nico Taylor, with the good news. Nico played on the 17 and Under Dallas Mustangs team the previous summer, automatically earning him a spot on the 18's team. He and Michael would play together again. The Dallas Mustangs' schedule was one of the most competitive in the nation. We were told that most of the college recruiters in the area followed their games knowing that the Mustangs were loaded with talent. With the importance of knowing where Michael would play the summer ball after graduation was a huge burden removed. Now he could concentrate on playing his very best ball as a senior.

Chapter 8
Mansfield Timberview High School

Michael attended Mansfield Summit High School as a freshman. He played on the freshman baseball team. He was a catcher on a team that wasn't very good at all and was poorly coached. I can't remember what the head coach's name was, and I had little respect for him. He did not follow select baseball and was unaware of what players on his team had played select baseball in the area. For the most part, high school coaches attend select baseball tournaments and get a glimpse of what talent is coming their way. This guy was only interested in the extra money he was earning as a teacher, which included coaching the freshman baseball team. Now, the varsity coach was well thought of and would attend freshman games. One day in the middle of the season, he made a point to come up to me and introduce himself and let me know how well Michael was playing and that he would be counting on him to help the varsity team get better. That was music to my ears. It was becoming hard to stomach as the end of the freshman season came to an end, but not before one of the players used a racial slur toward the only other African American player on the freshman team. That player wasn't nearly as talented as he thought he was, more mouth than anything else. I remember the kid's dad trying to deny his son would ever do something like that. You had the parents taking sides. I just wanted the season to end.

    There was a huge issue that came up concerning redistricting because a new high school was set to open the following fall in Mansfield. We lived in the most northern area of Summit High School district. The most southern area was known as the Country Club area of Mansfield High School. One of those areas would be realigned to the new Mansfield Timberview district. All along, the Country Club area was to be the area added to the new Timberview district. There were heated debates at all the Mansfield board meetings between the two areas. The Country Club area knew that Timberview was projected to have 68 percent minority enrollment. They would have to leave Mansfield High School that had a 13 percent minority enrollment. The politics that followed made it very clear hell would freeze before the Country Club students would be sent to Timberview. When the final redistricting was complete, our area was added to the Timberview district. We were numb and very unhappy. Also, Michael would have to play for a new school with a new baseball program. One Sunday afternoon, the summer before Timberview would open, Michael and I visited the campus. The baseball field was in place, but not complete. We walked on the field, and I told Michael I believed he would do some great things on that field. After that day, we always thought positively that everything would work out just fine.

Michael's first year at Timberview was quite eventful. As a sophomore, he tried out for the basketball team and made the team. I went to their first game and was shocked when he was introduced as the starting point guard. Although he had played basketball on the freshman team at Summit High the year before, it was a huge leap to varsity. Michael started 18 straight games. Although he played basketball, his primary sport was, as always, baseball. We knew it was inevitable the day would come that Michael would stop playing basketball.

The inaugural varsity baseball season was quite eventful. New head coach Robert Owens was a hard worker that prepared his team to compete with many question marks a new high school would have. Timberview won their first home game. Michael hit the first home run at the new Mansfield Timberview field. It was hit approximately 400 feet while clearing a group of power lines over the centerfield wall. When the ball was hit, my mind went back to that Sunday afternoon when Michael and I made our first visit to Timberview's campus. How fitting for his high school baseball career to begin with a bang! Unfortunately, the team was young and lacking enough talent to be consistent. Besides Michael, there were two outstanding sophomores. After that, a few other players stepped up and helped the team win enough games to advance to the district tournament. It takes time for any high school to build a good program. There were three high schools in the city of Mansfield.

Mansfield High School had the most talent, and its baseball program ranked as one of the best in the state. The college baseball recruiters and Major League Baseball scouts followed their program. It would take years for Timberview High School to earn that kind of following. At the end of Michael's sophomore year, he earned first team All-District 15-4A catcher. We were very happy for Michael to get recognized for his outstanding play. The team won a one-game playoff for the right to play in the district tournament. Timberview lost two straight games and was eliminated.

The second season was more of the same. Michael decided to stop playing basketball, which allowed him to start baseball practice with the rest of the team. The three outstanding players were about all Timberview had to try and be competitive. Michael showed his versatility by playing second base, and he also pitched. Coach Owens was trying to insert players in the lineup that had certain skills, and that seem to help. Yet, it just seemed like there was never a consistent product on the field. A lot of the players just expected to get better by showing up. It never happened, and it was an embarrassing reality that the majority of the team did not come to the ballpark ready to play on game day. The coaching staff did everything to motivate players while having them look at the consistent play of the big three: Michael, Jacob, and Matt. Despite going to the district playoffs in his sophomore season, the same would not happen in his junior year. Michael ended up hitting .433 with six home runs, another solid season. He earned first team all-district at second base.

Michael's senior year was full of expectations, both personally and for the team. He was 17-years-old, and earning a college scholarship was his top priority. There was little thought given to the 2007 MLB Draft. We just did not talk about it. Academically Michael was on the A-B honor roll with a 3.56 grade point average and had scored very high on the SAT. The huge obstacle was no recruiters came to watch Timberview High School. Although, Michael, Jacob, and Matt were outstanding baseball players, the rest of the team really struggled. What was even more disappointing was the fact most of the players had been on the varsity for three years. It was obvious many players did not care whether the team won or not, plain and simple. But the big three busted their tails every game and nearly earned Timberview a playoff spot with their outstanding play. Michael ended the season hitting .506, ranking sixth in the entire DFW area. He earned MVP District 4-5 A. You would think college baseball recruiters would have been lined up at Timberview to watch the three outstanding seniors. To the best of my knowledge and confirmed by head coach Robert Owens, only two recruiters came to Timberview to watch Michael play a game, Oklahoma and The University of Texas at Arlington.

Chapter 9
The Choice Family Proactive Approach

After Michael and I returned from the Southeast Top Prospect Camp at the East Cobb Complex in Marietta, we decided that Michael would provide me a list of the top 25 colleges he would like to attend to play baseball. He created a cover letter for each school, letting them know of his interest. Along with that letter we included Michael's biography and personal information and a ten-minute DVD featuring his baseball skills. The video included hitting, pitching, catching, infield, outfield, and base running. One of our very good friends we met while Michael played for the Dallas Giants, Ira Tobolowsky, created and edited the DVD. He did an amazing job, and we really appreciated everything he did. His work was outstanding. Twenty-five colleges received a glimpse of Michael Choice the baseball player.

Included in that group of colleges were most of the schools in the area. We received nicely written letters from a few schools, invitations to their baseball camps from the majority, and no response from the balance. As a parent, I personally felt we examined every possibility to ensure Michael would have opportunities to further his education. I desperately tried to understand the college recruiters and why my son was not being considered. First, I understood Timberview was not a stellar baseball program, yet what about his overall stats at the top of the list of prospects. His academic performance was well above the requirements. I did not want to think that race was a factor, but what else was I to think? Jacob signed to attend Arkansas, and Matt signed to attend Sam Houston State. Michael was still unsigned and the big question was: Why?

Approximately four weeks before Michael's graduation, on a Sunday morning, I knocked on Michael's bedroom door. He sat up in his bed and said, "Yes, Dad, what is it?" I suggested that we send out more letters and DVD's. He said, "No, Dad, everything will work itself out." He flopped back down on his bed. I went back down stairs with a smile on my face, convinced my son was right. I sat at the kitchen table enjoying the fresh brewed coffee my wife had made.

Nearly a week later, Timberview head coach Robert Owens told Michael that a UT Arlington recruiter had contacted him and made plans to watch him practice and play in the last two games of the year. As the story was told to me, a rival coach from Mansfield Summit called UTA's recruiter and told him he needed to take a look at Michael Choice. Shortly after, we received a call from Jeff Curtis, UT Arlington's head coach at the time, inviting us to a baseball game at UTA's campus. Thirty minutes before game time, after talking with us about their baseball program, Coach Curtis made a scholarship offer to Michael. It was a very happy moment and a refreshing end to a long frustrating search.

In the Timberview library, Michael signed his official letter of intent to play baseball at UT Arlington. Me, my wife Charea, and Michael's good friend and teammate, Jacob House, attended the signing.

After graduation in May 2007, Michael began playing summer baseball for the Dallas Mustangs. Wow! What a summer. This was the most talented team Michael had played for. The first three games, Sam Carpenter had Michael playing second base and hitting in the 7-hole. The fourth game, Coach Sam put Michael in the 3-hole, and he stayed there the rest of the summer. The Mustangs played a very competitive schedule. They had great pitching, solid defense, and a lineup without any holes. Michael hit for average and with power. Like most select baseball teams, the schedule was league games during the week and tournaments on the weekends. One huge tournament was the East Cobb Yankee Classic in Atlanta. The competition was all the best 18-year-old select teams in the nation. The venues were outstanding, highlighted by two games played at Georgia Tech. Michael played an outstanding tournament, hitting three crucial home runs. One he hit at Lassiter High School when the Mustangs defeated the East Cobb Yankees, 8-7. It was a long blast hit over the left-centerfield wall. Watching that ball disappear over the

Georgia pines was another Kodak moment. Nico Taylor also had an outstanding tournament, hitting a couple crucial home runs also. The Taylor and Choice family fondly reminisce about that baseball trip that was full of excitement. Many of the Taylor family made the trip to Atlanta from Dawson, Georgia to see Nico play and enjoyed watching Michael and the other Mustangs defeat the best teams in the nation.

Coach Sam would proudly tell parents that every player who plays for his team receives Division I baseball scholarship offers. And sure enough, as promised by Coach Sam, while the season played out, all the larger universities in the southwest inquired about Michael. Coach Sam responsibly informed all recruiters that Michael had signed with UT Arlington. Since Michael had not enrolled on campus, we were approached by several junior colleges that provided pipelines to big baseball programs. They would tell us about the schools interested in Michael. Quite a few schools admitted they received a letter and DVD from Michael, and some just admitted that they dropped the ball.

It was music to my ears to know that several big baseball programs that watched Michael play that summer knew what a good player he was. We were thrilled Michael was headed to UTA. His opportunity to play on the big stage for the Dallas Mustangs prepared him for college baseball.

Chapter 9
The University of Texas at Arlington

UT Arlington is located in the middle of a residential area in Arlington. Its baseball stadium is configured with the centerfield fence located approximately 40 yards from the intersection of Fielder Road and Park Row. Nostalgic is how I'd describe Clay Gould Ballpark, home of the UT Arlington Mavericks, compared to other Division I baseball stadiums. With residential homes in sight beyond the fences, it gives the ballpark unique character. I retired from the Aerospace industry after 29 years in June 2010. For years my normal driving route home would take me past the stadium. When the season was under way, I'd notice if games were being played. As I approached the traffic light, it was common for me to strain to try to read the score of games being played. I never envisioned my son playing for UT Arlington. I had taken Michael to games at UTA when he was younger so he could see the talent level required to play college baseball and the speed of the game on that level.

Michael enrolled at UTA in the fall of 2007. As a family, we were very happy for Michael. We always said openly, whatever school he ended up attending was destined to be. Although this was the only Division I scholarship offer he received, we felt it was a blessing, especially considering only a few high school baseball players were fortunate to play on the top collegiate level. For our family, it was an added bonus because we live 20 minutes from Clay Gould Ballpark. We would never miss a home game. Michael was always a hard worker on the field and in the classroom. We knew he would continue down that path at UTA. The first semester he lived at home, commuting to campus daily. When fall practice started, it was especially tough on Michael because weight training was at 6 A.M., and we lived close to 30 minutes from campus. The coaches locked the door to the weight room at precisely 6 A.M. If a player was late, he was not allowed in. Michael was never late prompting one of the senior players to point that out to those players that were habitually late, that if "The Infant," Michael's appointed nickname due to his young age when enrolling, could get there on time living off campus, there was no good reason for them to be late living near the weight room. Michael was 17 at the time, prompting him being pegged "The Infant." The previous year, the UTA baseball team had a reputation of a partying group of beer drinkers that had a horrible baseball season. Darin Thomas was named the new head coach after Jeff Curtis resigned to pursue a career in Real Estate. It was clear that the new leadership was determined to change the overall character of the team. Every player was held accountable for their actions on and off the field.

As fall practices progressed, I asked Michael how everything was going. His answer was always the same, "Fine." What position are you going to play? "I'm not sure. They have me at second base and outfield. The coaches are debating where I could best help the team." When they had scrimmages, Michael played all over the field. I could not get an absolute feeling just where he would play. My last question was whether he felt he'd get much playing time. His answer was, "I should."

The last hurdle was how would Michael do in the classroom. I worried unnecessarily. Michael had always been a good student. Perhaps observing how much work was required on the field and in the weight room, I wondered how that could affect his academics. He had made the A/B honor roll. After the Christmas holidays, baseball began its team preparations for the spring in January, with the first game of the season just weeks away.

Finally, it was Opening Day. I was nervous all morning like I had to play. By afternoon, my stomach was in knots. With opening pitch scheduled for 3:30 P.M., I arrived early for all pre-game warm-ups and batting practice. This was all breath-taking for me to watch, a routine that would be repeated for next three years. During batting practice, I observed Michael hitting with the group of hitters that seem to be starters. He was hitting line shots to all fields.

When infield/outfield warm-ups were done, it was clear Michael was going to be in the outfield.

As the starting lineup echoed loudly throughout the stadium by the public-address announcer, I was speechless! Michael was leading off and playing center field. After asking Michael many times where he was going to play was finally being answered. How very proud I was to see he was taking full advantage of his one opportunity to play major college baseball. Michael had an outstanding game, both offensively and defensively.

Coach Thomas was so impressed with Michael's first few games that he moved him to the three-hole in the batting order. His ability to knock in base runners kept him in the three spot his entire collegiate career. The first tournament UTA played in was hosted by Dallas Baptist University held at the Texas Rangers' Double-A affiliate (Frisco RoughRiders) at the Dr. Pepper Ballpark in Frisco, Texas. This tournament would give everyone a glimpse of what kind of collegiate player Michael would become. He went 9-for-19, a .474 batting average with five RBI. UT Arlington beat Southeastern Conference powerhouse Alabama twice, 10-0 in the first game led by Michael's offensive punch. He earned All-Tournament Team honors.

Michael had an outstanding freshman season leading UTA in all triple-crown categories batting .376 with seven home runs and 51 RBI. He also earned Southland Conference Freshman of the year, All-Southland Conference second team, Rivals.com Freshman All-American, first team National Collegiate Baseball Writers Association Freshman All-American, second team Baseball America Freshman All-American, Louisville Slugger/Collegiate Baseball Newspaper Freshman All-American, and Ping!

Freshman All-American. It was a storybook for everyone to see, including our family. It was if he set out to prove everyone wrong. I've always told Michael it is okay to play the game with a chip on your shoulder. He is a tremendous competitor.

Two games were very special to me during Michael's freshman year. The first was a game at Oklahoma, and the other was at home against Texas A&M. In the Oklahoma game, Michael hit a home run late in the game, nearly giving UTA a huge road victory. The recruiting coordinator for OU told Michael his senior year of high school in a telephone conversation, "Go to a junior college in the fall, have a good baseball season, and I'll reevaluate you next year." That conversation devastated Michael that evening, especially since I encouraged him to call OU to see if there was any interest in signing him after watching him play in a high school game two weeks earlier. As I watched Michael hit the ball deep over the right-center field fence, I noticed the obvious displeasure of that assistant coach as he left the top step of the OU dugout and sat on the bench after watching Michael's bomb disappear in the darkness. His body language suggested to me that he knew he had blown it as recruiting coordinator regarding Michael Choice! I drove back home from Norman that night with a smile on my face the entire drive. My thoughts were, "Evaluate that, OU coaching staff!" Later in the season, Michael had a monster game against Texas A&M at Clay Gould Ballpark. He went 4-for-4 with a home run, double, and a season-high five RBI, helping UTA defeat the then No. 7 ranked team in the nation. That was the only sold-out game I witnessed at home. Texas A&M's head coach, Rob Childress, gave a post-game radio interview, where he praised UTA's victory and was asked specifically what he thought about Michael Choice. He said, "He is one of the best position players I have ever seen. His presence at the plate is that of a senior. He has speed and power, I'd love to have him on my team." I kept that sound bite on my PC the entire year. I'd listen to it frequently to hear Coach Childress talk about my son. Michael was selected to five Freshman All-America teams and was named the Southland Conference Freshman of the Year. At the UTA All Sports Banquet, Michael received the Athletics Department Newcomer of the Year trophy, making his freshman year a complete success.

Scout day is held before the start of the season, usually during fall practice. It was clear that Michael would be looked at often and by all Major

League Baseball organizations in preparation for the June draft in 2010. From the first game, it was very noticeable the number of scouts present. Many wore their organization's logos proudly. Some carried briefcases or backpacks that were dead giveaways. Often they sat together as a group, openly discussing players, trading notes with each another. There were many times they would come up to my wife and I to say hello and introduce themselves or just making small talk. MLB organizations are very thorough evaluating prospects. We were contacted in the fall by the director of scouting for MLB to tell us that Michael was overlooked as a high school senior in 2007, but would not be under the radar in the 2010 MLB First Year Players Draft. We could not avoid looking ahead as parents with high hopes that Michael would fulfill his dream of getting an opportunity to play professional baseball. Often I wished I could fall asleep, wake up, and 2010 MLB First Year Players Draft was here. That was interrupted with the reality of a heavy schedule of games. My other concern was for Michael to remain injury free. He played the game hard and often made diving catches from his center field position. As a parent, I learned to relax and understand Michael stayed in the best physical shape and that was all he could do. There are intangibles that define the best players. Michael possesses many of those traits that help him produce on the highest levels. As a young player growing up, I would tell him, "You step up and help your team win! Don't look around for your teammates to get the job done. You do what is necessary to win!" That advice he used well and more often than not, Michael found himself right smack dab in the middle of outstanding performances, either up at the plate with a clutch hit or in the field defensively making a game saving catch. I can't tell you how many times other parents would speak to me after games saying, "Michael played a great game today." I would always say thank you. However, in the back of my mind I'd think, that is what he does! Perhaps if every player approached the games the same, how much better would the team be? That season's UTA team often had multiple players stepping up with outstanding performances. Michael is only human and occasionally would have a sub-par game. He rarely would go two or three games without a base hit, yet there were games where he would have multiple strikeouts. I'd always tell him that going down swinging the bat was much better than taking a third strike, allowing the umpire to control his plate appearance.

Michael always had a good eye. From an early age, he rarely swung at pitches out of the strike zone. That served him well for the most part, but most amateur umpires are horrible with inconsistent strike zones. I coached Michael to eliminate bad umpires by doing damage early in the count when possible. Once you get two strikes, then you give the umpire an opportunity to hurt you by ringing you up. Nevertheless, Michael would get his share of strikeouts by umpires. It is part of the game. Another bit of advice I gave Michael early on in his career was to keep an eye on the opposing pitcher while sitting in the dugout. By paying attention, you are able to see all of his pitches, location, and speed. When on deck, take practice swings on every pitch. Once up at the plate, you are as ready as you could be to win the battle against the pitcher. This is a habit Michael uses today to increase his opportunity to be successful with every at bat. There is no magic to becoming the best baseball player you can be. It takes hard work and listening to coaches giving solid advice. You cannot wake up one day and possess the required skill level to be a five-tool baseball player. Yes, you need to have God given talent to be among the elite baseball players. However, if you have a tremendous work ethic, are hungry for knowledge, and desire to pay attention to detail, it is very possible to be successful playing on the highest level of baseball.

For every young baseball player, getting to the top of the mountain seems to be an impossible task. The congestion of players thin out as time goes by. Many are not willing to pay the price for success. Some realize they will never develop the required baseball skills to play on the highest levels. Lastly, when you don't have the talent required, someone is being paid to tell you face-to-face you simply aren't what they are looking for. One has to face reality when that happens and move on in life.

Michael's second season at UTA quickly eliminated any thoughts of a sophomore jinx! He picked up right where his freshman year ended, playing with a chip on his shoulder every game. Michael established himself as one of the best baseball players in the Southland Conference and the nation as well. His signature attribute as a tremendous competitor was ever so apparent early on as UTA had an outstanding hitting lineup. Michael was well protected in his usual three-spot in the batting order with senior outfielders Matt Otteman (cleanup batter) and Andrew Kainer (5-hole) batting behind him. The opposing teams could not pitch around Michael. When they did, Matt and Andrew would make them pay. That season, UTA clearly proved they could play well against every opponent. Michael was hitting extremely well to all fields and with power. His accomplishments continued to increase his sophomore season. Michael finished in five Southland Conference top statistical categories, including second in on-base percentage (.492), fourth in batting average (.413), fifth in runs (64), fifth in hits (93), and eighth in slugging percentage (.644), and became the sixth UTA player in program history to hit for the cycle going 4-for-4 (triple in the first, double in fifth, single in sixth, home run in eighth) with three runs and five RBI against Northwood (4/21). He batted a team high .417 (20-for-48) in 12 games against ranked opponents with five doubles, one home run, and nine RBI. He also batted a team high .433 (29-for-67) in 17 games against opponents who made the NCAA Tournament. Believe me, there was more: he hit .459 (50-for-109) with 31 runs, eight doubles, two triples, four home runs, and 30 RBI during 27 games played at Clay Gould Ballpark, hit .371 (43-for-116) with five doubles, one triple, seven home runs, and 22 RBI during 29 games played on the road or at a neutral site, hit .406 (52-for-128) with six doubles, one triple, six home runs, and 24 RBI in 32 Southland Conference games, batted .367 (18-for-49) in 12 career games against Big 12 opponents with 11 runs, six doubles, three home runs, eight walks, and 15 RBI, hit .412 (14-for-34) against left-handed pitchers, and hit .414 (79-for-191) against right-handed pitchers, batted .467 (35-for-75) with runners in scoring position and batted .414 (36-for-87) with two outs; was second on the team with 25 two-out RBI, 12 multiple games, and with 30 multi-hit games, posted a team high four-hit games and finished with seven three-hit performances, ended the season on a season-high 12-game hit streak (May 1-May 22) batting .500 (23-for-46) with 17 runs, four doubles, two home runs, and 12 RBI, went 2-for-5 with a double, home run, and three RBI against eventual national runner-up and then-No. 4 Texas on the road with a game-tying two-run double in the eighth inning and a solo home run to give the Mavericks the lead in the top of the tenth inning (2/24).

That game was one of the best games I watched my son play. To watch Texas head coach Augie Garrido slam his ball cap on the floor of their dugout, after watching Michael give UTA the lead with his long homer to center field. Michael earned first team Southland Conference outfield and second team American Baseball Coaches Association South Central All-Region (OF).

It's Hard. But It's Fair

Three weeks before the Southland Conference Tournament, Michael received an invitation to try out for the 2009 USA National Collegiate Baseball Team. It was the greatest honor any college baseball player could receive. Forty-two of the very best college players in the United States would compete with each other to make the 24-man roster. Ten pitchers and fourteen position players were chosen after three weeks of practices and approximately twelve intra-squad games starting the second week of June. After UTA was eliminated from the SLC tournament, Michael worked out daily with his teammates in preparation for the USA National Team tryouts. After dropping Michael off at DFW International Airport, I realized he was going to experience a once in a lifetime opportunity. I visited the USA website and glared at all the talented players invited to the tryout. The list of invitees clearly represented most of the big player names and huge conferences in the nation. Like in the past, Michael never gave me any indication how the tryouts were going. He only talked about how dominant the pitchers were, most clocked in the mid to high 90's on the radar gun. I noticed from the box scores from the scrimmages that pitchers were dominating. As the three weeks of training camp was winding down, I started to get my little speech together to tell Michael there was no shame in not getting selected to the National Collegiate Team. It was clearly an honor just to get the invitation. Deep down inside I knew Michael would give his very best effort and would compete until the very end. The last week of training camp, his bat came alive. I received a call from one of our advisors, Jim Schwanke, that Michael hit a long home run over the batter's eye in straight away center field. Jim said that it was the buzz throughout the North Carolina training facility! Everyone was asking, who is that kid from Texas, from some small D-I school? Michael told me that after the last scrimmage, every player would get a final interview where their fate would be revealed. All forty-two players were instructed to pack-up all their gear and wait for their interview. If you were not chosen, vans were available to take you to the airport returning you to your hometown. That afternoon, Michael called me to say, "Dad I made the team." I darn near fainted! Caught completely off guard, I was speechless! How very proud we were that our son would be so fortunate. This would put Michael on the biggest baseball stage imaginable. Michael had told me early on in training camp that 50 to 100 MLB scouts were present at all the practices and scrimmages.

Charles M. Choice

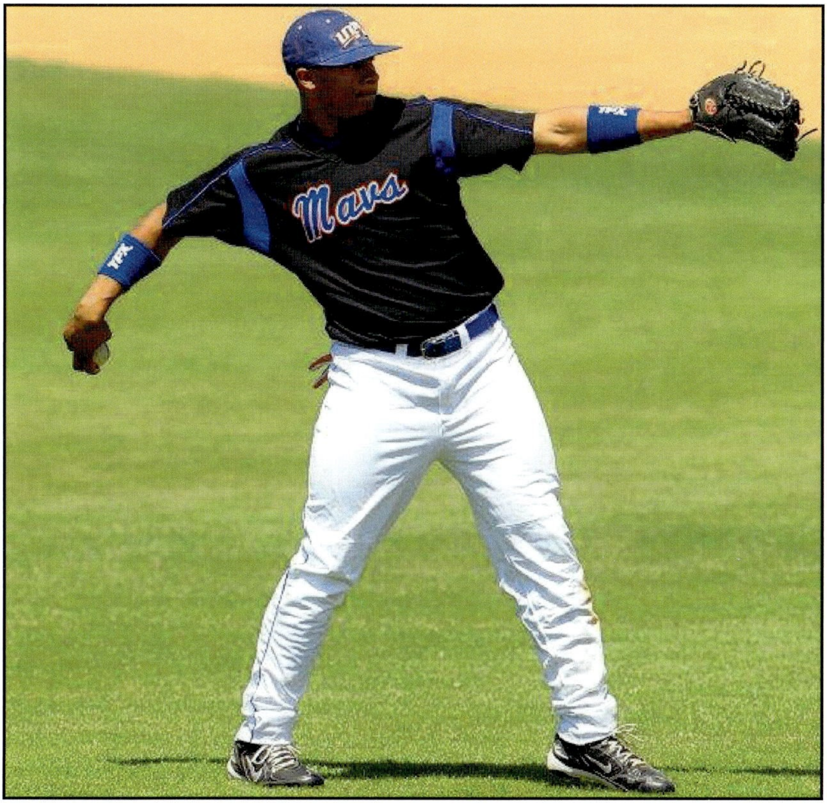
Mavs

MICHAEL
CHOICE
USA
BASEBALL
JUNE 25-JULY 26, 2009

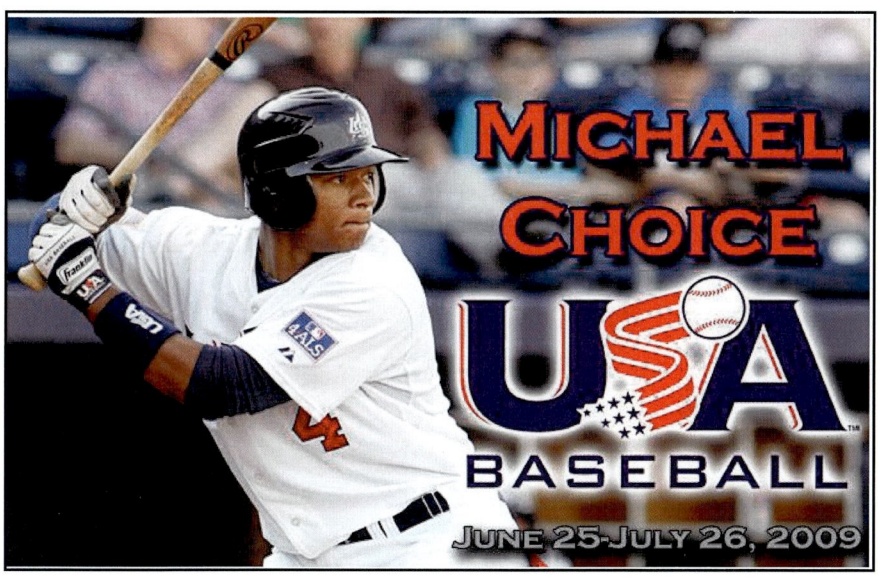

What that meant for Michael was phase two of a life changing experience. The 2009 USA National Collegiate Baseball Team would play several games in North Carolina against Team Canada and The Guatemala National Team. They would fly to Boston and play several games against Cape Cod League all-stars. While in Boston, the team took batting practice at Boston Red Sox' Fenway Park. Michael hit one over the "Green Monster" in left field, hitting one ball high up on a lighting structure! From Boston, the team flew to Toronto, then non-stop to Tokyo. While in Japan, a week the USA National team played in several cities against Japan's National Collegiate Team, Michael called home as often as he could to tell us about the breath-taking scenery and the awesome competition between the USA and Japanese teams. From Japan, they flew non-stop to Vancouver, British Columbia.

The USA National Team would play The World Baseball Challenge at Prince George, British Columbia, against national teams from Canada, Germany, and the Bahamas. The USA team won the tournament. Michael made the All-Tournament Team and won the top home run award with three home runs for the tournament. When Michael arrived home, I knew right away he had returned from a life-changing journey. He understood he was one of the best collegiate baseball players in America. He had competed with the very best against the very best. What better way to go into his junior year at UTA? After completion of his third collegiate season, the 2010 MLB First Year Players Draft would be held June 7. Unfortunately, the aircraft company I worked for was on strike, so as a family, we were unable to travel to North Carolina for the games Michael played with Team USA. I followed the box scores and featured articles from each game played. Nevertheless, we were very disappointed not being able to support Michael's dream opportunity representing our country as a member of the 2009 USA National Collegiate Team.

Michael's junior year at UTA was quite eventful with many breathtaking baseball highlights. Yet, no one could have accurately prepared our family for the many distractions we would experience. Now Michael, on the other hand, stayed calm and focused on the baseball field. He was challenged in every possible way. UTA lost 22 players from the previous year's roster and would be forced to play many inexperienced players. With the 2010 MLB Draft scheduled for June 7, there were no less than 25 scouts at every game. Michael was obligated to fill out in-depth paper work furnished by every MLB team.

Charles M. Choice

In between scheduled games, he worked out for the majority of the MLB organizations, hitting and fielding at the UTA field. He took it all in stride and concentrated on playing at the highest-level possible. No longer below the radar, opposing schools pitched around Michael from the first game. If the game was on the line, they simply walked him whenever possible. It was both frustrating to Michael and for our family, as well as UTA faithful fans. Yet, this year's team was remarkable in so many ways. The incoming group of freshman played well all-season long. It was as though they were not aware that many did not expect them to play on such a high level. Personally, I believe Michael's quiet leadership pushed them to follow his lead as a hard worker and fierce competitor. He would make the opposition pay every time they allowed him to hit. For this reason, I believe his third year was perhaps the most impressive year at UTA.

Despite all the distractions, he accomplished some very lofty achievements, including leading the nation NCAA (D-I) in walks (76), second in the nation in on-base percentage (.568), led the Southland Conference in batting average (.383), and became the all-time home run leader (34) in UTA history. Michael reached base safely in 72 consecutive games dating back to April 28, 2009, reached base safely in all 60 games in 2010, and during the final 12 games in 2009. In fact, dating back to his freshman season, he reached base safely in 118-of-120 games. In 166 career games, Michael reached safely in 157-of-166 games. These are only a few of the accomplishments that Michael achieved during his last season at UTA. His plate discipline of being patient clearly defines what a smart baseball player he truly is. The frustration of constantly being walked intentionally never seemed to affect his overall game. Defensively he made many outstanding game-saving catches in center field. Again I was reminded of the many Kodak moments we witnessed, where someone would shout out, "Did you see that!" One of those Kodak moments was a conference game in San Antonio against UTSA. Michael hit one of the longest home run recorded at the UTSA ballpark. His home run landed on the rooftop of an on-campus building located approximately 50 yards beyond the left field fence. It was estimated the ball traveled near 450-500 feet. The second Kodak moment was at Baylor Ballpark in Waco. In the first inning, with two outs and with two strikes, Michael hit a towering blast over the scoreboard structure in left-center field. It was perhaps the furthest ball I ever saw Michael hit. More important to me was Baylor was one of the schools Michael most wanted to attend. He had produced brilliantly in their team baseball camp with the Dallas Giants during the summer of 2006, yet was overlooked by their coaches. His home run was like icing on the cake, considering the Mavericks defeated Baylor the day before. One of the most intriguing things about Michael's patience at the plate is his ability to hit safely with two strikes. I recalled turning to my wife after watching the ball soar over the huge scoreboard in left-center field, asking her, "How does he do that with two strikes?" The fans barely got situated in their seats when you heard this thunderous blast where their outfielders never moved! In that game, Baylor would not pitch to Michael the remainder of the game, as he was walked in two of his following at-bats.

Michael received the following honors and awards after his junior year: Howard Green SABR Metroplex College CO-Player of the year, third Team ABCA/Rawlings NCAA Division I All-America, third Team National Collegiate Baseball Writers Association All-America, first Team Baseball America All-America, first Team Yahoo! Sports All-America, first Team ABCA South Central All-Region, and second Team Ping! All-America, 2010 first Team ALL Southland Conference (OF), 2010 Southland Conference Player of the Year, 2010 Southland Conference Hitter Of The Year, 2010 Southland Conference All-Tournament Team, USA Baseball's Golden Spikes Award Semifinalist (Top 30), and UT Arlington Baseball 2000s All-Decade Team (OF).

The three years Michael played for UTA went by so fast. He had some great teammates. He made friendships that will last a lifetime. We were privileged to attend every home game. We were thrilled so many times by outstanding performances and now that his college career is over, we are left with the terrific memories. Watching our son mature into a man and maintaining the high UT Arlington academic standards were very gratifying for me and my wife. We understood how much of a grind student-athletes have while attending college. We never took any of that for granted. Michael worked hard and took his one Division I scholarship offer and made the very best out of it. I like to say he took lemons and made them into lemonade. We always said that the university that would sign Michael is where he was destined to go. We would never second-guess anything. Why would we? Michael had a wonderful college baseball career at UTA.

UTA took very good care of Michael. His scholarship percentage increased each year. Most people are unaware that Division I baseball scholarships are radically different from football and basketball. NCAA Division I baseball programs only have 11.7 scholarships to divide among approximately 35 players that will make up the team's spring roster. Full scholarships, which are common in other collegiate sports, are almost never even an option to offer in baseball. Michael's percentage was very fair, but never 100 percent. We were blessed and like other parents, supported our son financially throughout his college career. Coach Darin Thomas always greeted our family warmly and would always say, "If you or your family need anything, just let me know." I told him that he was in powered to be Michael's dad when he was on campus or out of town on baseball trips. Our family had total respect for the coaching staff and UTA officials. I have always noticed the transaction section of the sports page of our local newspapers. They will identify student-athletes who are disciplined for breaking team rules or suspended from the team. Parents trust the coaches to run a clean program, demanding the student athletes to be responsible for their actions. We never have had any problems with Michael. When other parents would tell us what a respectful young man he is, that was always very gratifying to us. We enjoyed hearing comments like that more than how well he played in a baseball game. His makeup as a person will serve him well as he moves up in professional baseball.

Chapter 10
Michael Choice
Through the Eyes of Scott Lacefield

SCOTT LACEFIELD, UT ARLINGTON SPORTS INFORMATION DIRECTOR (2008-10)
When I took the job as Sports Information Director at UT Arlington, a big reason why was to work with the baseball program. I had played baseball under Mavericks head coach, Darin Thomas, at Seward County Community College (1998-2000) when Thomas was an assistant coach. It didn't take long for Thomas and his two assistants, Jay Sirianni and K.J. Hendricks, to start telling me about their top player. I remember asking K.J., "What is it that makes Michael Choice so special?" He laughed and said, "Everything!"

So needless to say, I was very excited to get to meet him, but also see him play.

Looking back, when I was on campus for my interview in the spring of 2008, Michael's freshman season, I saw him play a few innings against Baylor and remember seeing him after the game, and I was just amazed at his size for a true freshman.

For the start of the fall season, I wanted to do a one-on-one Q & A with Michael. I thought this would be something great for the UTA website and for its fans to hear about what Michael had been up to over the summer, along with getting some commentary from the program's Freshman All-American from the previous year.

I had heard he was a little quiet and reserved as far as his personality was concerned. So, I also wanted to get more acquainted with him because I knew we would be spending a lot of time together over the next two years. When I mentioned the idea to Thomas, he told me I would be the one doing most of the talking. So, I was really interested as to how this would go.

I met with Michael at the UTA Athletics offices at the CR Gilstrap Center, and we went to the conference room. We sat down and then started the Q & A. Michael was very relaxed, but it was obvious that he wasn't a big talker. He was humble, and you could tell from the expressions he made and his body language when I started asking him to talk about his success during his first college season that he wasn't all about himself.

I knew he didn't mind talking about it, but he always quickly changed the direction of the conversation back to something revolving around the team. He didn't want to focus on himself. I also remember Mike saying that he was just concentrating on trying to be a starter during his freshman season. I'd say he accomplished that.

Michael was named to five Freshman All-America teams and led UTA in all three Triple Crown categories (.376 batting average, 7 HR, 51 RBI). In fact, his .376 batting average marked the best ever by a UTA freshman.

That fall season, UT Arlington played TCU in a game at Lupton Stadium in Fort Worth, just a scrimmage for the two teams to see what they were looking like for the upcoming year.

Michael Choice was the show, I do remember that much. I wasn't able to stay long, as I was also working volleyball that fall season. In the first game, Michael went 3-for-3 and in his first at-bat of the second game hit a scorching line drive over the center fielders head for a double. I started getting a feeling this kid was for real.

Once his sophomore season started, you could tell he was pressing a little bit at the plate because he felt there was quite a bit of weight on his shoulders to carry the team. The previous year, UTA had a pair of seniors who had good seasons with Danny Slinkman and David McLeod, who were both gone for the 2009 season. But thankfully for Michael and the Mavericks, it didn't take long before two new seniors stepped forward to help fill those gaps.

Senior outfielder Matt Otteman and senior outfielder and designated hitter Andrew Kainer both had phenomenal seasons in 2009. In fact, Otteman hit .432, Kainer hit .417, and Michael batted .413. It marked the first time in school history that three Mavericks had all hit over .400 in the same season.

It could be argued that UTA had the best outfield (when Kainer would play left field and not DH) in the entire country. The thing about it is even though these three players were playing at a smaller NCAA Division I school, I was convinced that all three could go hit in the middle of the lineup at any school in the entire country.

And when you talked to scouts and other coaches, they would all tell you the same thing.

Michael was a star, plain and simple. Kainer had perhaps the most impressive run during the 2009 season as he not only hit .417, but also broke the Southland Conference hitting streak record with a 36-game hit streak. Otteman was named the Metroplex Player of the Year while hitting .432 with nine homers and tying the school record with 58 RBI. And Otteman also had his own hitting streak to be proud of, a 26-game streak that tied the then-school record before Kainer broke the record later in the season.

So, Choice was protected in the lineup with Otteman hitting four-hole and Kainer hitting five-hole. The problem for the Mavericks offense that season was even though the team had a .300 batting average (thanks to The Big 3), only those three mentioned players actually batted over .300. But, I have to admit, I don't know if I had ever seen a murderer's row quite like that where any of the three players could hurt you at any minute like they could.

Early in the year, there was a lot of talk among the baseball world that Michael would have a great chance to make Team USA, or at least get the invitation to the trials. Many know just being invited to tryout is a big deal.

Michael was one of the initial 17 that were invited while 36 of the top collegiate players in the country ended up making the trip to Cary, North Carolina for the trials.

Most of the time, there aren't many small school players that are invited to try out for Team USA. As the start of the 2009 season rolled around, I was hoping that Michael wouldn't be overlooked. In fact there had only been one player in the Southland Conference's history that had ever been invited to try out for Team USA. And nobody from UT Arlington had ever had the opportunity.

Just like Michael did so many times during his career, he made history and was invited to try out. I just knew that once those people saw his abilities, like all of us lucky ones that got to see it every day, it would be a no-brainer for them to keep him on the Team USA squad for the remainder of the summer.

I will never forget walking up to Clay Gould Ballpark the day we found out he had been invited. I wanted to go out and talk with Michael and get some quotes for the release that I was going to send out to announce his invitation to Team USA.

And what better way to describe Michael, I walk out to the field and can't seem to find him. He wasn't in the dugout, he wasn't in the soft-toss area, and I knew he was there because any time Michael told me he would be somewhere at a certain time, it was a guarantee, he was going to be there.

Low and behold, I look across the field, all the way over into the left-field line bullpen (home side of the field at UTA is the first base/right-field side), and I see Michael mowing the grass in the visitor's bullpen.

There is the Freshman All-American and now Team USA invitee over at UT Arlington's Clay Gould Ballpark mowing the visitor's bullpen grass. I'm telling you, that is just Michael. He is down to earth, he doesn't view himself as bigger or better than anyone else, and he never looked for special handouts.

I started talking to him, and you could tell he was excited, but never did he make it seem like this was just supposed to happen. He was very gracious for the opportunity. He never felt he was going to be handed a spot on the team. He knew there was a job to be done once he arrived in North Carolina for the start of the tryouts for Team USA. He knew he had to prove to them all that he belonged with the best players in the country.

And a great side note on that day, the same day he was announced as going to try out for Team USA, Michael became the sixth player in UT Arlington history to hit for the cycle. He went 4-for-4 with a single, double, triple, and home run in the Mavericks 23-7 win over Northwoods University at Clay Gould Ballpark in Arlington. And I know one thing, that home run, the last of his four base hits, is without a doubt one of the hardest hit baseballs I have ever seen. He hit an absolute missile straight over the left-field wall.

Following the 2009 season, Michael headed to North Carolina for the start of the Team USA Trials. I would talk to Michael every week or every two weeks just to get an update, as I was doing a daily report on www.utamavs.com to give fans an inside look at what was happening with Michael. Because when you think about it, this was the first time a UTA player was getting this opportunity, who knew when the next time it would happen.

Michael would tell me how unbelievable the pitching was at the trials. I knew there would be good pitching, but I also knew Michael was one of the best hitters in America. No doubt about it. Michael tore through Big 12 pitching and other strong non-conference opponents just like he did Southland Conference competition.

I remember one time after playing TCU, the Horned Frogs coach, Jim Schlossnagle, said he would have rather pitched to Babe Ruth in a certain situation than have pitched to Michael Choice. Schlossnagle and the TCU program are one of the best in the nation. Due to its proximity, the Mavs and the Horned Frogs would play several times during the year and even that one fall season over in Fort Worth. So, to hear these compliments from a coach like that, I had no doubts Michael could compete at the highest level possible in college baseball.

Michael was one of several position players who were struggling at the plate during the team trials, but then all of a sudden, he got hot. He hit a home run and then a day or two later, he finished the trials going 2-for-4 with a single and a double. I just knew he would make it. There couldn't be five to six better hitters in the country, much less 10-13.

Then the news came, he made Team USA! Little did he know, but that would end up changing his life.

Michael had an incredible summer playing for Team USA. All of the honors, stats, and prestige that you could ever imagine, Michael was receiving them all. Michael was hitting in the middle of the lineup for the best collegiate team in the nation. They were beating teams in Japan and Canada, and Michael was a big part of the team's success.

I remember I was at the airport once that summer, and I was talking to K.J. Hendricks, one of the assistant coaches for the Mavericks, and my roommate on UT Arlington baseball road trips. He had taken a trip back east to see Michael with our head coach at UTA, Darin Thomas.

They went to see Michael just after Team USA's trip to Boston when the team had taken batting practice at Fenway Park. K.J. was telling me about the batting practice session Michael had at the home of the Red Sox, and how he was hitting baseballs halfway up the light tower behind the Green Monster, the famous 37-foot high left-field wall at Fenway Park. Oh, and I forgot to mention, he was doing all of this WITH A WOODEN BAT!

So, when I was talking to K.J., and he was telling me all of these things and what all of these scouts were telling him, it made me ask him, "So what are you thinking this means for him and the draft next year?"

K.J. then told me what I wanted to hear, he said, "Oh, Lace, he is going to be a first-rounder, there is no doubt about it."

I was just so excited for Michael when I heard that. I knew by what I felt I had seen, there just couldn't be that many players out there who were better than Michael. Little did we know that he just kept upping his stock as the summer went along.

As the summer ended, Michael finished it in fashion as he hit the most home runs in the World Baseball Challenge, hit .350 on the summer with three doubles, three homers, and 13 RBI with a .453 on-base percentage and .550 slugging percentage. He led Team USA to the World Baseball Championship title while earning the Home Run Hitting Award (most homers at the tournament) and was one of four Team USA players named to the All-Tournament Team.

Then it all started, Michael was named the No. 8 professional prospect on Team USA by Baseball America, and all of the talk in the fall was about the Major League Baseball Draft.

I truly don't believe Michael had any idea of what was about to come his way. Whether he knew or not, he sure took it in stride like a true champ, like a true professional.

He never made any of the attention a distraction. He never made his teammates feel like he was above them or deserved special treatment, never. He was just a true pro from day one.

Pro scouts were at the UT Arlington fall baseball practices nearly every single day. And that is not what is normal in the fall. A scout or maybe two might come around for a practice just every once in a while, and then there might be 15-20 at the MLB Scout day that the program holds. But nearly every fall practice, there was at least one scout attending wanting to watch Michael's every move.

I was talking to Coach Thomas and also to John Mocek, the Senior Associate Athletics Director at UT Arlington who is a baseball historian, had worked at UTA for nearly three decades, and who played baseball at UTA and served as a coach for the Mavs for many years. Mocek was also an official scorer for Major League Baseball at Texas Rangers home games for over 11 years.

Both Coach Thomas and John Mocek knew what was in store for the spring and for the draft, you could just tell. Talking to both of them, they were both saying that when Hunter Pence, a current Major League All-Star, was playing at UTA, there were never scouts coming out to see him in the fall, and Pence was a second-round pick!

Both would just grin and shake their heads and say, "Lace, you just wait and see what this spring is like, it will be unbelievable!"

They were right!

And once again, you have this superstar in the making roaming the halls of his hometown university, cruising through campus with nobody really knowing who he is. Sure, his close friends from high school and even the ones he ran around with at college, they knew who he was, but I truly don't think anyone at UT Arlington or around the city had any idea of what kind of product this city had produced and who this young man was that was here playing at its university.

Of course, Michael never wanted to be noticed. He just wanted to be treated like everyone else. And he was just like everyone else, in a sense.

He hung out with his friends, he played video games, he listened to his iPod, he was one of the quietest, to himself players on the team, and he just enjoyed being around his friends and teammates. The last thing he ever wanted to do was being noticed more than anyone else on the team.

I will also never forget one of the times Michael was at my office. During his time at UT Arlington, we became closer and closer due to the time we would spend together with his media requests, photo requests, and obviously with all of the post-game interviews, etc.

So from time-to-time, he would come by my office as he was in the C.R. Gilstrap Center, coming by to see the coaches or swing by the locker room or do whatever. He would just come by my office, sit there, and visit for a few minutes or sometimes just sit in there and look at his phone.

One time he was there, and with my office right near the front door to the building, a college-aged kid, right around the age of Michael, walked in and was standing in the lobby. Michael just glanced to see who might have walked in as he probably heard or could tell the door had opened.

It was someone Michael recognized, so Michael went out into the lobby area to visit with him. I was able to overhear their conversation.

The person who walked in said, "Oh, hey, Mike, I didn't know you were going here (talking about UTA), what are you up to? Are you playing basketball here?"

Michael said, "No."

The other guy said, "Oh, are you running track?"

Michael said, "No, I play baseball here."

And at this moment, I'm sitting there with my jaw on my laptop as I'm just utterly amazed at the conversation that is happening with one of the best collegiate baseball players in the country with someone he went to high school with, in the same exact town as he is going to college.

So, Michael and the guy who walked in ended their brief conversation, and Michael heads back into my office.

Now, if that had been me that exchange happened to, I would be just amazed and would come back into the office and just go off on how I couldn't believe that guy didn't remember me, much less remember what sport I played.

Michael, on the other hand, comes back into the office, sits down, and I could tell he didn't know I was able to hear his conversation with the guy who, I had figured out from their brief discussion, had went to high school with him.

So, I said, "Who was that?"

Michael said, "Oh, some guy I went to high school with."

That is when I couldn't help it, I said, "And he didn't know you played baseball here?"

Michael, as he always would, cracked a smile and said, "I guess not, Lace."

And I just laughed and shook my head and told him that I couldn't believe that. He just laughed. Once again, I can't tell you enough how humble of an individual Michael is and how incredible of a person he is.

Working for a school that is a really small fish in a big pond like UT Arlington is in the Metroplex, it wasn't very often that a reporter outside of the school newspaper was in attendance at many UTA sporting events.

I was always trying to find unique story ideas to pitch to our local media to try and get some positive publicity for our programs at UT Arlington. Even with a talent like Michael, it was still difficult getting the attention of newspapers like the Dallas Morning News and the Fort Worth Star-Telegram. With four major professional sports in the area and with colleges like North Texas,

It's Hard. But It's Fair

SMU, and TCU surrounding UT Arlington, just getting into the papers for a small recap of the team's games was a major achievement at times.

But once Michael started his final season, the talk about the kid at UTA who is going to be a high draft pick started to pick up.

We had interview requests for Michael early in the year, mostly from national websites that focused specifically on college baseball. I remember Michael did a taped interview for a podcast for CollegeBaseball360.com, which wanted to talk to him mostly about his experience with Team USA. But it was also great for the UT Arlington program as Michael was obviously the face of the program.

A few more requests came in during the fall, but more than anything, I was filling out more and more questionnaires about players that we had who I felt belonged on preseason All-American teams. It didn't take much work as Michael's success spoke for itself, but I made sure and nominated him for every award under the sun, as I knew he had a chance to win each and every one of those awards. I knew it and everyone around Michael knew it, I just felt it was time for everyone across the country to find out what this Michael Choice kid was all about.

As the season came closer, Michael started having quite a few interview requests. If anyone was going to cover the team, anyone from a national publication to a school newspaper or radio reporter, all interview requests began and ended with asking for one specific person, Michael Choice.

There were even times that Coach Thomas, the head coach of the team, wouldn't be requested, but Michael would.

And with all of the distractions that were already presented to Michael, he never frowned upon doing any interview. It was amazing. After a long day at practice, maybe even if he had to leave early for class or after a good or bad game, I never had to worry about Michael turning down an interview. He was always very polite, respectful, and always professional and would always put the UT Arlington program and his team first while answering any and all questions the reporter would have for him.

He always made my job so easy. I don't think he will ever know how thankful I was that he handled all of those interview requests the way that he did.

As January came rolling around, Michael started having his name show up as several of the preseason conference and national awards began coming out.

I would always find out about the award and then I would text message, call, or just tell Michael when I saw him next to let him know about the awards as they were coming in. He would always have the same response, just a simple, "Thanks."

Michael was never wrapped up into all of the awards and honors that he received. I think he felt that they were nice and an honor, but I don't ever think that he was doing what he was doing on the field or working as hard as he was so that he could receive those awards and honors. I just think he loves the game and due to his abilities and skill level, those honors came right along with it.

I decided to put together an "UT Arlington All-Decade Team" that included all of the top UTA players from 2000-2009. This team would include one player at each position, along with a utility player, four starting pitchers, and a reliever.

As I was sitting there going through each and every player's stats from the decade, one player stood out among all of them. It was Michael.

Sure, UTA had numerous players from the 2000's that were deserving of the recognition, and several could not be named because of the number of good players at a specific position. But out of the true great players at UTA during the decade, none had started their collegiate careers at UTA and had the immediate success like Michael did.

One or two were also Freshman All-Americans, but they hadn't improved like Michael had. Several were drafted very high after their UTA days were complete, but they hadn't started their careers at UTA, they were JUCO transfers who came in at 20 or 21-years-old and had one or two outstanding years and then were off to the professional ranks.

There are good players, great players, and even players who help change the program. UTA has had several of all of those. Major League All-Star outfielder Hunter Pence played at UTA. Arizona Diamondbacks third baseman Ryan Roberts played at UTA and even Boston Red Sox pitcher John Lackey played at UTA, none of those players left the mark on the program like Michael Choice did. And that is saying something as both Pence and Roberts were Southland Conference Players of the Year. Heck, Roberts basically rewrote the all-time record books in his two seasons at UTA. But, like I said, none of those were like Michael.

And that is why naming Michael to the All-Decade team, a decade where he only played two of his seasons, was a no brainer. It was great watching all of the former players assemble at Clay Gould Ballpark to receive their awards, and there was Michael, in full uniform as UTA was preparing to play a game that day with the rest of the greatest players to play at UTA in the decade to be honored. It was a true sight. Because you could tell several of the former players were really taking a long look at this youngster, as they all knew there was something very special about him.

Being in the Metroplex, UT Arlington always seems to have a lot of scouts around the ballpark. As Big 12 teams would come into Arlington for a midweek series or for other schools in the conference to play the Mavericks in a weekend series, you would always see Major League Baseball scouts attending the games.

Then came the spring of 2010, if there was an MLB scout that hadn't been to Clay Gould Ballpark on the campus of UT Arlington, they were getting out the map and figuring out a way to be there for that spring season.

I truly couldn't believe how many scouts were showing up to watch "The Michael Choice Show" that spring. It was truly amazing. One time I counted 27 scouts that were in the stands or by the dugouts with two and a half hours before the first pitch of the game was thrown. Yes, two and a half hours before game time, and there were 27 MLB scouts at a UTA game.

They were literally watching Michael's every move. As the team stretched, they watched Michael. As the team jogged to center field, they watched Michael. As the team warmed up throwing in the outfield, they watched Michael. They were taking notes and keeping close tabs on everything that he did.

This continued for the first month of the season. Maybe not 27 scouts each game, but at least 10-15.

Then Michael got into the batting cage.

I have been around a lot of baseball and played through college. I have never in my life seen anything like what Michael Choice can do in a batting cage. The show that he puts on during batting practice is just a special sight to witness. And believe me, the scouts took notice.

The best way to explain it is the ball sounded so different when it would come off his bat compared to any other player. And I mean everyone. We could be playing Baylor, Oklahoma State, Texas, Oklahoma, or Texas A&M, as we always would throughout the year, and when Michael hit the ball, it made the rest of the players stop and watch.

It always made me laugh watching the other players on the team stop whatever they were doing to watch Michael take batting practice. But who could blame them?

All of the scouts would stop what they were doing and break out their camcorders or clipboards as soon as Michael would walk in the cage. As soon as he took his first swing, WHACK, they would just stay locked in, then another swing, WHACK, they wouldn't move. Then finally after his last swing, WHACK, the scouts would put down their camera or write their final bit of information and then subtly shake their heads as to say, "I can't believe what I just saw."

I was always amazed at how Michael went about his daily routine as normal as he possibly could, even with all of the scouts in the stands. He obviously knew they were all there, but you wouldn't have ever known it. He just went about his business, didn't over try, and just did his thing, which was such an amazing thing to see.

UTA had opened the 2010 season and played on the road for a couple games at nearby Dallas Baptist and then came a big road midweek challenge at Oklahoma.

We pulled into the ballpark, and I did what I normally did before the game. I went into the dugout and visited with the UTA coaches before waiting for the starting lineups. And this is a good three hours before the scheduled first pitch. As I got the lineup, I headed up to the press box, which at OU is very nice and spacious.

When I walked into the press box, I saw a gentleman sitting in the press area talking on his cell phone. I knew the Oklahoma SID, and that wasn't him, and I also knew their radio announcer, and that wasn't him either. I had no idea who this man was.

Finally, he got off the phone and asked if I was with the UTA team. I told him I was and immediately, he just flat out said, "Tell me about the Choice kid."

I knew at that moment this was a scout who was looking for some character background and possibly some information that other scouts/MLB personnel wouldn't be able to receive. So, I spent a good ten minutes talking on and on about Michael and just how great of a player he was and how he was an even better person.

It's Hard. But It's Fair

The scout sat there, just looking into my eyes while I was talking to him, before just nodding his head while saying, "That is pretty much what I have heard from everyone."

And I wasn't telling him any secrets, just what a dedicated, humble, and hard-working individual Michael was.

He also told me that Michael's makeup was off the charts. Makeup is measuring just about everything outside of a player's skill and talent, basically everything that makes the player who he is. Makeup is what a player is like off the field, how hard of a worker he is, what his personal background entails, etc. This scout had done his homework. He knew Michael. He said they were going to be one of many teams who were going to be very interested in him as the draft got closer.

More and more awards came pouring in for Michael, even throughout the season. He was named to the Baseball America mid-season All-American team, which was a huge honor. Not only had he met expectations with all of the pre-season awards, he had exceeded those expectations. His numbers at the midway point of the season were staggering: .393 batting average (42-for-107), 11 home runs, 31 RBI, 36 walks, .541 on-base percentage, and .766 slugging percentage in 32 games played.

Shortly after this, Michael was named to the Golden Spikes Award Watch List. Basically this would be like being named to a watch list for the Heisman Trophy. Here Michael was, hardly recruited out of Mansfield Timberview High School, and he was at little ol' UT Arlington, and he was now being grouped with the best players in the country for the Golden Spikes Award, a national award given annually to the top collegiate baseball player.

About the only problem Michael ran into during his junior season was something that was completely out of his hands; nobody wanted to pitch to him.

It is a good thing that he didn't have to come back for his senior season because they might have just walked him 220 times and not thrown him one strike because that is basically what happened during the 2010 season when he received 76 walks, a UT Arlington and Southland Conference all-time record.

Among his 76 walks were 21 intentional walks, a UT Arlington record. It was just amazing at what teams were willing to do while avoiding pitching to the All-American. I don't know how Michael didn't get completely frustrated,

I was up in the press box and I was frustrated, but he just took them all in stride and never, ever complained. Because, in the end, Michael was getting on base and giving his teammates opportunities to drive him in.

One thing that was being rumored around the UTA baseball program during the fall and even into the spring was something that took me a lot of time to actually believe. And then it happened. Michael was being rumored as being an option out of the UTA bullpen. Yes, I did just type that.

Michael has a very good arm in the outfield, and it turned out that he also had a good arm on the mound. This was something that the UTA coaching staff didn't want to have to entertain, but more than anything, Michael was the one telling them he was willing and ready to take on being the team's closer.

He even went as far as to writing "Mariano" on the dry erase board in Coach Sirianni's office, as to comparing himself to future Hall of Fame closer, Mariano Rivera of the New York Yankees. He would always grin and tell me, "Lace, you just watch, I will be the closer this year."

I just shook my head.

Well, in an off-season that included a few injuries to a few pitchers who were being counted on to pitch, Coach Thomas gave Michael the chance he was looking for, he headed out to pitch.

I couldn't believe what I was seeing, and I was just praying, "Please, don't let him get injured," as he went out to the mound for warm ups.

I have to admit, it looked like he knew what he was doing, at least a little bit. The Michael Choice pitching project thankfully only lasted two innings while he struck out two, walked four, and hit a batter, but I still give him so much credit for not worry about draft status or anything else, but just wanting to help the team. That was always his number one focus.

With all of the eyes that were looking at our box scores following the games to see what Michael had done at the plate, each time he pitched, I had numerous phone messages and emails telling me, "You might check your box score, there is a mistake, it shows Michael Choice pitched today."

If I had to say, just one part of his junior year that probably not many people will remember that does stick out in my mind, it was probably those two pitching outings. I still have some photos from those as evidence that it did happen!

It's Hard. But It's Fair

The Michael Choice show headed on the road to San Antonio, and this marked his first conference series on the road. I was made aware that Baseball America would have a photographer at the game. This was something special in itself. Baseball America doesn't just go around covering games. They do too much with the sport at all levels to be out covering games, much less a Southland Conference game. But what they were there to do was take photos of a future first-round draft pick.

This photographer was in attendance to do one thing and one thing only, take about a million pictures of Michael. His lens was glued to Michael from the moment he arrived at the ballpark, probably around 20-30 minutes before the first pitch.

His first at-bat Michael hit a laser to the shortstop for an out. His next time up, he grounded out to third base on the first pitch to end the Mavericks half of the third inning.

Then Michael gave not only the Baseball America photographer something to see, but everyone in attendance at Roadrunner Field. Michael led off the sixth inning, hitting a 1-0 pitch just about as far as you could possibly hit a baseball, all the way up on the rooftops of the dormitories way beyond the left-field wall at UTSA's home ballpark.

In a game UTA lost, that shot hit by Michael gave everyone in attendance something to talk about and something to compare to the furthest baseballs they had ever seen hit in that ballpark.

That day it started among all of the sports information directors that I would come in contact with. Most of the time we all know who the good players are on each team, but there is usually never a reason to ask about the individual players as they are usually just as good as the good players on your own team.

As I have mentioned several times before, Michael was different.

I'd say just about every SID I came in contact with wanted to know about Michael Choice. They wanted to know how he was to deal with, they asked how much attention he was receiving from scouts, and just wanted to know in general how he was dealing with all of the attention because it wasn't every year that a player in the Southland Conference was being regarded as one of the top players in the nation. And it seemed everyone knew he was coming off playing for Team USA.

We went to Northwestern State in Natchitoches, Louisiana where UTA squared off with the Demons and with their top pitcher, Luke Irvine, in the series opener on Friday night. In my opinion, he was without a doubt one of the top pitchers in the conference, a left-hander with a very good breaking ball.

The Mavericks won the series opener against Irvine, 3-1, while the Demons ace lefty struck out 11 batters in six innings, but Michael went deep, and the Mavs scored runs in the fourth, sixth, and eighth innings to win the game. I just remember this game/series because Northwestern was one of a very few teams that decided to pitch to Michael, I definitely respected that decision.

It was probably because the Demons had perhaps the best pitching staff, top-to-bottom, in the league. Michael made them pay though as he belted three home runs, including one off Irvine.

I remember one of Michael's homers on that Sunday, it sounded awful off his bat and was going the opposite way, as most of his homers that season went to the opposite field, and the ball just continued to carry and left the ballpark over the right-field wall. It was just amazing the power Michael displayed and really giving him an aluminum bat that season was just unfair. Michael's power made any ballpark seem small. Even Clay Gould Ballpark, the home of the Mavericks, which is without a doubt considered as a pitcher's ballpark.

Here he was just cruising through the season with 11 home runs and 30 walks before April even started.

I'm telling you, it was just amazing what was happening in front of everyone's eyes. Here he was, an All-American at UT Arlington and hitting in a batting order in the three-hole without a proven hitter behind him and just taking the few pitches that he was thrown and just hammering them. He was hitting baseballs as hard as I had ever seen them, almost every time up. Even the few outs that he did make were hit extremely hard.

A lot of times people will look back after a memorable period in their life and say, "I guess I never realized what was happening was as special as it really was."

Nobody was saying that with Michael, nobody at least that was around him on an everyday basis. Everyone one associated with the UTA program knew what they were witnessing was something they would probably never see again.

I had a lot of conversations with the coaches at UT Arlington, all of which had been around special players during their playing and coaching careers and just continued saying, "He is just a special player."

The head coach of the Mavericks, Darin Thomas, won a national championship coaching the Liberal Bee Jays in the National Baseball Congress summer leagues. While at UTA, he mentored Hunter Pence, Adam Moore, Ryan Roberts, and Mark Lowe while at UTA. All of those mentioned players are currently playing in the big leagues. Thomas also coached a handful of big leaguers in his time coaching summer baseball in Kansas.

Assistant coach Jay Sirianni, the team's pitching coach, played collegiately at Nebraska and grew up with big-league third baseman Casey Blake. Sirianni also played a couple years in the Cleveland Indians organization.

Assistant coach K.J. Hendricks, the 2000's All-Decade shortstop at UTA, played for the Mavericks before beginning his pro career with the Colorado Rockies. He played in the Rockies minor league system from 2002-2007. Hendricks was rated as the fastest base runner in the Rockies organization at one point and made it all the way to the Double-A ranks before his career was cut short due to injuries.

My point is the UTA coaching staff knows talent. They have been around and seen some of the best baseball players who have played collegiately and professionally over the last 20 years. They would always tell me, "Lace, you might not ever see a player as good as Michael Choice ever again."

It wasn't something that anyone who was around the UTA baseball program took for granted. We all knew we were watching something that was very special and something that doesn't come around very often.

Then came the shot heard around the world. Well, at least around Waco and believe me, it was a SHOT!

The Mavericks went down the road to Baylor for a midweek matchup with the Bears where Michael Choice most definitely left his mark.

In the first inning, just eight pitches into the game, Michael hit a ball that nearly everyone in the press box stated as the "furthest ball they had ever seen hit," and I was one of those people, as Michael hit a ball over the scoreboard structure at Baylor Ballpark that landed in the soccer field beyond the left-center field wall. Going off of the distance to the left-center field fence and guessing about where the ball would have landed after going completely over the giant scoreboard structure, many estimated the home run traveled between 450-500 feet.

Later in the season, we headed out to Corpus Christi, Texas for a conference series with the Corpus Christi Islanders. Michael was on the verge of breaking the school's all-time career home run record in just his third season with the program.

It was a perfect day for the Mavs, UTA clinched the series with a win over the Islanders in game two of the series, head coach Darin Thomas became the program's fastest head coach to win 50 conference games, and Michael broke the school's all-time career home run record with his 32nd career homer, his 14th of the 2010 season.

It was the top of the seventh inning, and Michael launched the first pitch he saw, a fastball, and way over the scoreboard in right-center field to make him the all-time home run king at UTA.

After the game, I went to talk to him to get his reaction and also to talk with some of his teammates and also to Coach Thomas, asking about Michael's achievement.

Michael said it really didn't even strike him that the homer was the record breaker until he rounded first base. I'm sure he was just doing what he always did, just worried about helping the team and trying to put a good swing on the ball, nothing special, just what he always did.

I talked to several of his teammates, all probably more excited about the monumental achievement more than Michael was, but all of them just saying over and over how happy they were for him and how hard Michael had worked to get to where he was in his career.

I think head coach Darin Thomas said it best; he told me, "Michael's best days of baseball are ahead of him."

How true. As excited as we all were looking at what he accomplished, which was no small feat, was just a small blimp on Michael's career radar that would lead to so many more great achievements down the road.

Michael started the season being projected by Baseball America as a first-round pick in the 2010 MLB Draft. The publication had him as the No. 30 overall pick in its preseason magazine. After the season got going and scouts started plugging in their opinions, Michael's stock started to skyrocket. Midway through the season and into April, people were saying they would be shocked if he was not in the top 15 picks.

More and more high-level MLB scouts and organizational general managers and cross checkers were coming around and now, as we knew he would be a first-round pick, we really started to pay attention to the indi-

It's Hard. But It's Fair

vidual clubs that were spending several days in Arlington to watch Michael's every step.

I think when it truly hit me the hardest is when the Cleveland Indians had its high-level personnel in town and when I mean in town, I mean they were around practice and just about everything baseball related for at least three days. A very extended trip to see Michael.

Right away, I was thinking, this is unbelievable. Cleveland has the fifth pick in the first round.

That is when I knew Michael would have his name called very, very early on draft day.

I can remember all of the teams that had top 10-12 picks all spending a lot of time around the UTA baseball program during the months of April and May. It wasn't a matter of if Michael was going to go early, it was now just who would be the team that would take him.

Michael was breaking records, he was hitting home runs, and he was doing just about everything. I remember one time there was an internet scouting guy in attendance, one who basically creates his own content, provides it here and there to some national scouting services, but really just wanted to come get some video of Michael playing and probably post it on his website. He was harmless as far as I was concerned.

But I remember him really wanting an in-depth interview with Michael following the game, as he was leaving town after the Friday-night game of the Mavericks series against Stephen F. Austin.

We were now into May, and the season I felt like was possibly starting to weight a little bit on Michael. Just simply because of all the pressure he was under, all of the evaluations that he had to do, and just with knowing the draft was only about a month away. And more than anything, for Michael, he was really trying to help UTA win and to improve their seed in the upcoming conference tournament.

So, this media member had asked me if he could do a big interview with Michael following the game. I remember asking Michael and of course, he said no problem.

I remember the game was a pitching duel, a really well-pitched game by UTA starter Jason Mitchell (one of many by him that season) and also by the SFA starter. UTA won the game 1-0.

Michael went 0-for-3 in the game with a pair of strikeouts and a walk. Teams were not pitching to him and when they were, he would on occasion get a little anxious and chase a few pitches out of the strike zone from time to time. This is nothing that isn't normal to every college baseball hitter in the country.

So after the game, I went down with a few reporters who were at that game and this reporter who was expecting this in-depth interview with Michael.

I knew Michael was happy because of the victory, but I also knew all of these reporters wanted to talk to him, even though he went 0-for-3, as they always did. They just wanted to hear from the star, even though he didn't get a base hit in the game.

I went up to him and said, "Are you sure you feel like talking to these guys right now?"

He looked me straight in the eye and said, "Lace, I'm fine."

And he sure was. He handled all of the questions and analysis of his swing from the one reporter who had filmed every pitch thrown to him during the game with complete class. Just as he always did.

That reminds me of a moment with Michael I will never forget.

Monday was always the team's off-day for all of its players. It would be the day they would get caught up on homework or even just a day to relax and do laundry after a long road trip from the previous weekend.

The UT Arlington student radio station had started broadcasting a few home games and one of their broadcasters, Kyle McGuinn, had asked me if he could do a one-on-one interview with Michael in studio on a Monday afternoon. He said it would be no longer than 15-20 minutes.

I told Kyle that during the spring there were no promises for a request like this on an off day, as I knew this was the one time during the week players were not expected to be up at the facility or at the field preparing for the upcoming game. So, I just told him, no promises, but I would see what I could do.

I was completely upfront with Michael about the request, and I shouldn't have been surprised when he said, "Sure, that's no problem."

So we headed over to the UTA radio station, and Kyle did an outstanding interview with Michael, focused on the team, on Michael's individual success and honors, and even went back and talked quite a bit about his time with Team USA.

It's Hard. But It's Fair

Before we all knew it, Kyle had conducted a 45-minute interview with Michael.

In a way, I felt horrible. Here is a guy who has no free time and when he does, he is probably filling out questionnaires from Major League Baseball organizations or talking on the phone to someone about all that is going on with his future, and he just gave a 45-minute interview with the school radio station on his one off day during the week.

What a class act. But I wasn't surprised, that is just how Michael is. I did tell him though, this is only going to help you as you move down the road in your career with being comfortable talking to the media and doing these kinds of interview requests. He understood and was happy to do the interview with Kyle. And I will also admit, Kyle did a great job doing his homework and just had topic after topic lined up for his interview with Michael, both enjoyed doing it.

One of the most amazing things I witnessed with Michael on the field was his ability to reach base safely. Not just hitting line drives all over the field, but also with his patience at the plate and the ability to draw walks. Obviously receiving 21 intentional walks also benefitted this skill set, but Michael, who also has speed, worked his way on base over and over and over again. Michael was also able to reach base with an infield hit, as he would always get out of the batter's box well and get down the first base line.

He finished his collegiate career-reaching base safely in 72 consecutive games. This isn't just getting on base with an error or a fielder's choice. This is reaching safely on a base hit, walk, or hit-by-pitch. And think about it. If a hitter lines out, pops up, and grounds out in a game, a streak like this might be over. Michael was able to reach base safely in every game during his junior season (60 games) and during the final 12 games of his sophomore season.

In fact, Michael reached base safely in 118 of his last 120 games played at the college level. Only twice in 2009 did Michael not reach base safely. In his career at UT Arlington, Michael reached base safely in 157 of 166 career games.

The end of Michael's junior season came with even more awards. It was literally a shock if we went two straight weeks without Michael receiving some type of honor. And I mean national honors. During his time as a collegiate player, including his time with Team USA, Michael received a total of 59 honors and awards. This is truly remarkable. And just think 40 of those honors came during his time as a junior at UT Arlington in 2010!

There was no doubt that Michael was the best player in the Southland Conference and if you asked coaches around the league, they would tell you the same thing. But there is always something a little screwy with all-conference voting within the league and with the league's coaches. Not just the Southland Conference, this is with all conferences. Sometimes the coaches will just let their sports information director fill them out, or sometimes the coach will just vote for players that play on the teams of the coaches they like the best. It is truly just hit or miss on how accurate those teams are sometimes.

And with the Mavericks finishing fifth in the league, I was personally a little worried that a player from the first-place team or a player who might have lead the league in wins on the mound might get the nod as player of the year. Luckily I didn't have to worry long, as Michael was named the conference's player of the year and hitter of the year. Very well deserved for Michael.

What also helped Michael along the way was how he handled himself on the field. He never made it about him and was never a show off or what some people might call a "hot dog." Michael went about his business just like any other player on the field. When he would receive walk after walk with opponents refusing to pitch to him, he would toss his bat to the side and jog down to first base. Never made a show of it.

With the end of the season near, that also meant the Major League Baseball Draft was getting closer and closer. As much attention as Michael received during the season and in the weeks leading up to the draft and as much talk was always going on around the team, it was truly amazing how it never seemed to bother or affect Michael or his teammates.

I started receiving a lot of phone calls and emails from people around Major League Baseball, primarily the people who were handling draft coverage and from college baseball insiders who were constantly wondering who was going to draft Michael. A lot of the people were just looking for a way to get insider information on who was all talking to Michael and who were the teams that were most interested.

And like I mentioned, it wasn't if Michael was going to be a first-round pick, it was now which organization in the top 15 picks was going to select Michael.

It's Hard. But It's Fair

Everyone had his or her opinion. And in baseball, it is very difficult to predict the draft as all of the players drafted go directly to the minor league organization. Other sports you can look at teams' rosters and see where they have specific needs. In baseball, each organization will usually take the best available player/pitcher at the spot where they draft.

But a lot of the teams were doing their homework. Michael talked to every organization and had one-on-one time with clubs, so they were obviously noticing that he would be an excellent fit with any team that decided to draft him.

I had bloggers that cover so many of the MLB teams calling and asking for interviews with Michael. The ones who were connected to MLB.com, I granted access to interviews with Michael before I would a blogger or someone who wasn't connected to a reputable organization.

I remember when we were at the Southland Conference Tournament in Corpus Christi, the final games of the season. Michael had been invited out to the MLB Network headquarters for the MLB Draft Show. Harold Reynolds and Kevin Millar personally made phone calls to Michael to see if he was interested in attending the show in New York.

Michael politely declined, explaining his family and close friends would be watching the draft show from his home in Grand Prairie.

That week we were in Corpus Christi, I think I had somewhere between 8-12 requests for interviews with Michael. As much as I wanted Michael to have even more exposure, I really had to be careful to not make all that was happening become an even bigger distraction to Michael. Because more than anything, Michael wanted to see his team, the UT Arlington Mavericks, have success and advance in the conference tournament and to hopefully win the tournament and advance to the NCAA Tournament.

I want to say we did 3-5 of those interview requests and just explaining to the others that Michael was concentrating on helping the UTA baseball team in its postseason tournament and only had time to do a few of the interview requests.

Because when you really look at it, all of the players had very little time in the morning before they were expected to attend a team breakfast or go over to the field to watch some other teams play. Or the players were then getting prepared to go to the field to play. Then after games, obviously most players would want to relax, enjoy a meal and time with their families or just go back to the hotel and do something to take their mind off baseball.

That is why it is even more impressive that Michael did as many interviews as he did.

Many of those media members understood the situation, others, of course, were upset that their requests were not met. The interviews I lined up for Michael he did, as he always would, a great job with and spent a good amount of time talking to about his situation with the draft and what all he was expecting.

It was also interesting how "Michael Mania" had reached just about everyone in attendance at the conference tournament. When we were walking in the hotel lobby, he would be signing autographs. When he was walking around the concourse of the stadium, people would stop him to have him sign autographs.

I'm sure Michael got used to this during his time with Team USA. We would always sign a bunch of autographs, even after home games at UTA where there were maybe 250-400 people in attendance for most home games.

On June 1, 2010, Michael was named a semifinalist for the Golden Spikes Award, the top honor in college baseball. He was one of 30 players in the nation that were named to the semifinal list. Once again, as this seemed to be the theme for the 2010 season, this had never been done before by a UT Arlington player. Michael was the first. What an honor.

Before we knew it, draft day was upon us. Monday, June 7, 2010, and the entire world would soon be learning a little bit more about Arlington's own Michael Choice.

The Choice family planned a gathering for many of Michael's childhood, high school, and college friends, along with many of his family members from the area. This party also included several of Michael's teammates from UTA, along with the Mavericks coaching staff and many of Michael's previous coaches were in attendance as well.

My responsibilities for the day started weeks in advance. I knew this was going to be a once in a lifetime situation for the UTA program, so I wanted to make sure that nothing was left out of our coverage, but also promoting Michael to the local and state-wide media.

Perhaps the most overwhelming but least demanding access that I worked with was the MLB Network. The all-baseball all the time network had just a few players that they sent TV crews out to their specific locations to document all of the happenings on draft day. Michael was one of those players.

The crew that the MLB Network brought was large (at least ten individuals), but they knew exactly what they needed to do to set up and to get everything ready for their "live shot" that would come as soon as Michael was selected.

My main concern was making sure we had as large of a local sports media presence as possible. As I mentioned before, it was always a huge struggle to try and attract our local Dallas-Metroplex media to what was happening at UT Arlington.

In my two years at UTA, the Mavericks defeated a top-10 ranked opponent in 2009 (No. 7 Baylor) in Arlington, defeated another Big 12 opponent that same year (No. 17 Oklahoma) at home, had a player break the Southland Conference record with a 36-game hit streak, and had Michael Choice, who was the best collegiate baseball player the Metroplex had seen in years. And this includes any program in the Dallas/Fort Worth area.

And yet, it was always difficult to know for sure you were going to get coverage, even from something as large as this was going to be for Michael, a local product, and for UT Arlington.

So I was busy weeks in advance, contacting our media (both TV and print) about the event that the Choice family was hosting for the night of the first round of the draft.

Many of the local media were interested, but as it always goes, they just couldn't commit because they just said they never knew what was going to happen on that day. I understood, but as I told them, "We are going to have a player drafted in the top half of the first round of the Major League Baseball Draft."

When the day came, I was pleasantly surprised how many media ended up showing up. We had media from four of the five major television stations; we had a representative from MLB.com, Dallas Morning News, Fort Worth Star-Telegram, UTA's school newspaper, The Shorthorn, and a few other media that made their way to the gathering.

Of course there had to be one TV station that gave me the excuse that they had to cover Tony Romo, the Dallas Cowboys quarterback, as he was trying to qualify for the U.S. Open Golf Tournament. I don't even remember what I replied to that phone call with. I wasn't happy, I can tell you that. Every other major television station in town was there, so that was fine with me.

MLB Network had a truck with a giant satellite, along with a crew that would have made you think the Choice residence turned into the MLB Network studio. They were very professional and made every effort to stay out of the way with the rest of the party that the Choice family was hosting. But with the lights, microphones, and cameras, it was hard not to make it seem like a huge production because it was!

Michael was his typical self, just very relaxed and seemed like he had a game plan for what was all about to unfold. He was playing video games with some friends when I arrived, some four hours in advance of the actual start of the first round.

I brought our UTA backdrop for the interviews that would take place, immediately after he received the phone call from the organization that drafted him. I also brought printed materials that documented all of the coverage of Michael throughout the season along with notes, stats, and just about everything else that gave all of the information of his unbelievable season and career at UTA.

What I thought was funny was out of all the material that I brought with me, the one piece of material that was used the most was all of the mock drafts that were coming out. I printed out what I felt like was the 5-6 most reputable and provided everyone who wanted one the information that the so-called experts were saying about the draft.

These materials showed Michael was projected to go anywhere between No. 8 and No. 15 in the first round.

As I mentioned before, we were all just so excited that we just knew for sure he would go in the first round.

Before 2010, the highest drafted player in UTA history was Hunter Pence, who the Houston Astros drafted in the second round (No. 64 overall) in the 2004 draft. Another thing I was keeping an eye on was former Louisiana-Monroe pitching star, Ben Sheets was the highest drafted Southland Conference player of all-time as he was the No. 10 pick by the Milwaukee Brewers in 1999.

I knew Michael had a shot at becoming the highest drafted Southland Conference player in history, but at the same time, I really didn't care as long as it was the right situation for Michael with the right organization.

I also made sure that our coverage, UT Arlington athletics, was second to none as I brought two of my student workers, Phillip Long and Josh Bowe, to help with all that we were going to produce.

It's Hard. But It's Fair

Phillip took care of all our video responsibilities. He had a flip camera and started filming as soon as the draft began as I wanted an up-close reaction of Michael, his family, and everyone when he was selected.

Josh took care of our live blog on the website (utamavs.com) that provided up to the minute information as people were coming into the home and as the draft started giving pick-by-pick details. Both Phillip and Josh were huge assets for me that day as I was trying to communicate with our media to help direct them to the house and also giving information about Michael as many of the media members had never even seen him play. Hard to imagine, but true.

Most of the media were asking for and wanting to know the exact time that he would be drafted and by what team. That was probably the funniest part. I was able to tell them it will be in the first 15 picks probably, but as anyone knows, drafts are very unpredictable and as players are taken one-by-one, it changes how the following teams make their selections.

Back to the party.

The Choice family truly rolled out the red carpet for all of their guests. You could tell this wasn't their first go-around on hosting a party. The food that they had, oh, my gosh, it was just unbelievable. Mrs. Choice had some help, as some of her family was there to help prepare the food. But I'm telling you, the spread that was out that day could challenge any that has ever been prepared before. And I'm even talking about Thanksgiving spreads or anything of the sort. This family truly did a top-notch job on making that gathering one that nobody in attendance would ever forget.

Michael's family had the perfect home to host an event like this. The living room was basically spread apart at the seams for the MLB Network as they had to position all of their equipment to best get Michael in the picture for when the draft started and for when he heard the commissioner call out his name. Michael was positioned right in the middle of the room, he had his mother and father on each side of him with several other family members and close personal friends in chairs right next to him on both sides. Behind Michael and where ever else they would fit was everyone else in attendance. This included just about anyone who was close with Michael. I was able to position our television media and our camera and video media on the border of the windows and in chairs just in front of the television and around the couch in the living room that faced Michael as he sat in the middle of the room facing the family's big-screen television.

The house also includes a stairway that starts towards the back-middle of the living room and starts to wrap upstairs, so this also allowed more people to look in on all the action. It was amazing. I would bet there were close to 60-80 people coming in and out of that house during the day.

As the draft was about to begin, MLB Network's producer gave a few instructions, nothing major, basically just told everyone to be as quiet as possible as Commissioner Bud Selig made each announcement of who was being drafted for each pick so they would have the shot of Michael and his reaction as his name was called.

It was just so exciting for each and every person that was there. It was exciting for a number of reasons, first off, just thinking of the stage that this put Michael on was unreal and how this was the start of his professional career. And also for the entire country to hear a top draft picks name followed by The University of Texas at Arlington.

From that point on, more than likely, when you mentioned UT Arlington baseball to someone, they would immediately follow with, "Oh, that is the school where Michael Choice played."

More than anything, every person in attendance was there to support Michael. Everyone was just so incredibly happy for him because of the kind of person he is.

The draft began. The first pick was Bryce Harper, a high school-turned junior-college player who was the talk of the draft, nationally, in the weeks leading up to the first round. That was about the only pick that everyone knew was locked in.

Picks two and three were more than likely going to be a high school pitcher and high school shortstop, and either really could have gone second and third overall.

Now is when things started to get really interesting. As the Kansas City Royals, Cleveland Indians, and Arizona Diamondbacks were coming up with the fourth, fifth, and sixth picks.

From what I knew, Kansas City was a long shot for Michael, but with it being a small market team, they were a possibility as every team positioned in the first half of the first round knew Michael wasn't going to cause problems

It's Hard. But It's Fair

with being sign-able, which every team needs to know before selecting a player; they need to know exactly what the player is looking for as far as a signing bonus is concerned.

Michael was up front with all of the organizations, immediately letting them know he would be willing to sign for the amount of money that is associated with the position where he was drafted; he was willing to take "slot money."

With that being said, the Royals selected Christian Colon, a shortstop from Cal State Fullerton, and one of Michael's teammates from Team USA in the summer of 2009. Colon would end up being the first player in the first round to sign on the dotted line, proving there were no signability issues there.

This is when everyone in the house started to get really excited. Everyone close to Michael and the program knew the Indians had shown a ton of interest in Michael during the entire season and sent just about everyone in their front office down to Arlington to spend a lot of time with Michael to evaluate every last detail.

Obviously, with only four players taken, there were still several high-profile players left on the board to be taken, and the Indians went with Ole Miss left-handed pitcher Drew Pomeranz, another one of Michael's teammates from Team USA who nearly every mock draft had going in the top 4-8 picks.

The Diamondbacks were up next and at this point, everyone was just sitting there, waiting and waiting for Michael's name to be called. Minutes seemed like hours at this point as we were all starting to get nervous, excited, and just ready for Michael to have his wait ended with his name being called.

Then the Diamondbacks threw the ultimate curveball by selecting Texas A&M right-handed pitcher, Barret Loux, with the sixth overall pick.

This is what I was talking about. Drafts are very unpredictable and although Loux was a very highly touted prospect, there was nobody who saw him going this early in the draft as he was being labeled as a possible No. 15-20 pick.

So, this pick is what shuffled things up for the teams who would follow.

The New York Mets, which was the one team in the top ten that really didn't ever seem truly interested in Michael, selected right-handed pitcher Matt Harvey with the seventh pick. Harvey was out of North Carolina University.

With the Astros, an in-state organization, up next, people in the room started to get really excited and a bunch of people started making the comments, "Can you imagine, both Michael and Hunter Pence in the same outfield!"

91

Those people were thinking about both UTA players someday playing for the Houston organization. That wouldn't be the case as the Astros, somewhat surprisingly, took high school second baseman Delino DeShields Jr., son of former big leaguer Delino DeSheilds, with the eighth overall pick.

Most experts had DeShields Jr. going in the first round, but much closer to the middle of the round.

So eight picks in, everyone in the house was now waiting on egg shells, especially with two surprises and now two teams coming up that everyone knew had a lot of interest in Michael.

In the week leading up to the draft, Michael took a trip out to San Diego to not only workout for the organization, but to get a little closer look at the city of San Diego and of the organization.

The Padres picked ninth. So a lot of us thought this would be the spot Michael would go in.

In the back of a few of our minds was Jeff Curtis, the former head coach of the UTA Mavericks who was now scouting for the Padres and actually had the Metroplex as one of his areas. As much as he told everyone the organization loved Michael, he informed us that the organization would likely take high school right-handed pitcher Karsten Whitson (Chipley High School in Florida) if he was available in that spot. So it seemed like the Padres were thinking of taking Michael here because, in their minds, Whitson would have already been taken by possibly the Diamondbacks, Mets, or Astros.

Well, because Loux and DeShields went where they did, Whitson, the high school pitching prospect, was still on the board, and that is whom the Padres selected at ninth overall.

When Selig announced that pick, you could hear the anxious feeling leaving the room.

Not necessarily disappointment, but just a feeling that maybe that was where he would go.

Now all focus in the room went to Oakland. This was an organization that everyone knew had interest in Michael, and we were being told from several sources close to the organization that if Michael was available at No. 10, they would be taking him, no questions asked.

Obviously with Michael growing up where he did (Arlington), it had always been a dream of his to play for the hometown Texas Rangers. The

Rangers, who had also said if he was available at No. 15 would take him in a heartbeat, wouldn't get that chance because with the 10th pick in the 2010 Major League Baseball First-Year Players Draft, the Oakland Athletics selected Michael Choice from The University of Texas at Arlington.

The room erupted with excitement and joy as Selig called out Michael's name and out of all the people in the room, by far the calmest of them all was Michael. As excited as he was, you could just tell he knew there was business left to be done, as he knew he would be going on live with the studio crew at MLB Network after the selection had been made.

It was a moment that I will never forget. As Selig called out, "The Oakland Athletics select Michael Choice..."

The Choice household went crazy! It was a very special moment and one that I will cherish for the rest of my life. Just a great, great feeling and just so happy for Michael and his family.

Michael, as he always did for two years with me, did an outstanding job with his interview with all of the people on the MLB set.

Once Michael completed his on-air interview and was mobbed by his friends and family and shook hands with nearly everyone in the room, he went outside where I had the UTA backdrop set up, and he answered all of the questions from the local media.

All of the questions came firing at Michael.

"What does this mean to you?"

"What are your thoughts as your dreams came true today?"

"Was it a relief when you heard your name called?"

"How does this feel to put the UTA baseball program out there on a national level?"

"How does it feel knowing you are going to be coming back home while playing for the A's in the American League West?"

"What are the challenges that are now placed in front of you?" And so on and so on.

Michael handled all of the questions as professionally as possible and was first-class. I definitely couldn't have asked for him to do any better with the media than what he did on draft day, especially considering all of the emotions he was feeling.

To do what Michael did during his final season at UTA was nothing short of remarkable. Every team we faced pitched around him. He didn't have near the support in his own lineup as he had as a sophomore and just knowing what was on the line with the draft, he handled all of those issues and performed like a champion each and every day.

Everyone knew Michael was not going to drag out negotiations with whoever drafted him. So, I'm sure the Athletics organization was pleased to know their first-round pick was going to be a player they would be able to sign rather quickly.

With how things work on signing bonuses, nobody ever wants to be the first one because everyone is waiting to see what the player in front and behind them signed for. This created a little bit of a wait for Michael, who I know was more than ready to start playing professional baseball.

I saw him around the athletic offices quite a bit during June and July, and I was always asking him, "Have you signed yet?"

He would just smile and say, "Not yet, Lace."

And like I said, it wasn't because of Michael, it was due to the process. He understood, and he waited and waited patiently.

Then came the end of July, Michael and Oakland finally came to an agreement on a signing bonus; Michael received a $2 million signing bonus from the Oakland Athletics. What a blessing this was for Michael. He is so deserving.

In my opinion, Michael was drafted by and signed with the perfect organization for him. But looking back, it almost makes me laugh considering the Padres, who picked ninth, passed on Michael to get Whitson, and they ended up not signing him, which sent Whitson off to college at the University of Florida.

Something must have happened that made Whitson unsignable, which I'm sure they were not happy with because there isn't an organization out there that would draft a player in the top ten picks that wasn't positive they would be able to sign him.

But, like I said, Michael, without a doubt, went to the right organization, and I know the A's are very happy with their selection of Michael Choice.

During the summer of 2010, I was offered a job as Associate Director of Athletics Communications at Texas Tech University during the middle of July, and I accepted the job in the days following the offer.

It is funny how timing works. On one of my final days in the office at UTA, Michael came by with a big smile, he told me the negotiations were complete, and he was going to sign with the A's. I was so excited for him.

And there he was, Michael Choice, the kid from Arlington who nobody

It's Hard. But It's Fair

knew about and nobody recruited, sitting in the UT Arlington Athletics Department with his paperwork for his $2 million signing bonus with the Oakland Athletics. It was a pleasure for me to be able to write that final press release of Michael's UTA career, while it also marked my final press release as a member of the UTA athletics department. In such a short time, what a name Michael Choice made for himself.

Michael went out with a bang, and I felt like getting to cover Michael and work with him for those two years are the highlight of my professional career, without a doubt. I have never worked with an athlete that has had the natural ability as Michael, but I can also say I have never worked with anyone as humble and gracious as Michael is either.

That is why when I knew I had the opportunity to work on this project with Michael's father, Mr. Choice, I didn't hesitate. It was my pleasure to be able to share just a few of the stories that I had with Michael and watching Michael from the fall of 2008 to the spring of 2010.

Michael Choice is a winner, both on and off the field. Anyone who has the chance to be associated with Michael during his career will be tremendously blessed along the way.

Chapter 11
Our Advisors Jeff Frye And Jim Schwanke

NCAA rules are put into place to protect the student-athlete and the university he plays for. The parents are permitted to have an advisor to interpret all the many rules that, if broken, could lead to loss of eligibility. The players are not allowed to have an advisor and for good reason. Players have enough on their plate with academic and baseball responsibility. Most people around college baseball are open and honest with everything. Yet, lurking right around the corner are savory type characters willing to cut corners. That is where having a good advisor pays huge dividends. Most advisors are affiliated with professional agencies. Our family was approached by several reputable agencies. We listened to each of their philosophies and how they would represent Michael. We chose Franklin-Frye Agency. Jeff Frye and Jim Schwanke came to our house the fall of 2009. After a thorough presentation, we determined they were the best fit for Michael. They stayed in direct contact with our family on a regular basis for two years. Their honesty and integrity was always above board. All the top-level scouts knew them, and we were able to receive first-hand information on what MLB teams were most interested in Michael and often when they were going to attend games. Jeff played in major league baseball for nine years. Jim coached at LSU for 16 years. Together they had a wealth of baseball knowledge to share with Michael.

During that initial presentation, both Jeff and Jim had very high projections for Michael regarding the 2010 MLB Draft. We were spellbound with what they were saying, "Michael would be a first round draft pick." Before predicting that, Jim said, "Through his contacts in college baseball, he was certain Michael would receive an invitation to try out for the 2009 USA National Collegiate Baseball Team." Every parent enjoys hearing good things concerning their children, and we are no different. Moving fast-forward at how all of this played out is almost unbelievable. Nevertheless, it all happened.

Michael was one of their clients. They had obligations with other players, yet both Jeff and Jim frequently attended Michael's games both at home and away for two years. I judge people more on what they do rather than what they say. It was clear to me that my wife and I have the best advisors possible. We knew that once the draft took place, Michael would have the best possible professional agency in Franklin-Frye.

During Michael's junior season with all the distractions, Jeff and Jim helped us keep our sanity. The area scouts, scouting directors, organizational cross checkers, and other high-level staff members representing MLB organizations knew Jeff and Jim. They talked with most of the organizations about who Michael Choice was and our family as well. Toward the end of the season, Jeff gave us a clearer picture what MLB teams were interested in drafting Michael. With two weeks before the June 7 draft date, it was projected that Michael would be a first round pick. There were several teams with late-round picks telling Jeff they did not believe Michael would still be available at the time they were slotted to pick. We remained calm because we knew and were prepared for anything to happen. It was very intriguing to look at all the mock draft predictions, but there were so many, you could get dizzy trying to keep up.

Michael understood that Jeff and Jim were advisors for me and my wife, and that was how it was. Yet, that whole situation is a charade by my opinion. The NCAA rules are a joke in many ways. You have college head baseball coaches making huge salaries and the players and families struggling to pay university tuitions and housing. Every year there are some players losing eligibility for breaking a specified rule.

Our family appreciated Jeff and Jim. Michael was very comfortable with them and that, to my wife and I, was the most important thing. From what we have heard from other families, some advisors don't spend enough time with them to build a good relationship. The larger agencies have large quantities of clients and can't find the time to be more supportive.

One week before the June draft, our family had dinner with Jeff and Jim to give us the latest information they had concerning Michael's projectability in the draft. The past two years had flown by so fast. They were very knowledgeable about our son the baseball player and the person. I'm convinced that they had done an effective job passing their knowledge on to most of the MLB organizations. I say this because multiple times MLB scouting personnel would tell us, "Jeff told us to go and talk with Michael, you'll see he is even better a person than baseball player. We did, and Jeff is right!"

MLB organizations invest millions of dollars signing players and because of this, they rely on their scouting department to be thorough in all areas. When you look at the success of the winning organizations, they will quickly give praise to scouting and player development.

Franklin-Frye Agency is relatively small compared to many, yet, we are convinced Michael's interest could not have been served any better. Jeff told me many stories how he had to "scratch and claw" as a player all the way to the big leagues. His mental toughness was always evident as I watched him interact with all of the MLB organizational members that we interacted with throughout those two years. I called it his "Jack Russell Terrier Approach." Lastly, Jeff told me personally, "Our agency will never drop Michael as a client because of a sub-par performance year." There aren't many agencies that will make that claim. Michael has a winner in Franklin-Frye Agency.

Chapter 12
2010 MLB First Year Player Draft June 7, 2010

Here it is! Draft day! We finally got to this date. Our family has looked to this date for such a long time. I'm especially on a cloud because I retired from the aircraft industry, after 29 years, less than a week before. We are full of anticipation, what team will draft our son? After reading all the mock draft predictions, who has got it right?

I'm an early riser, and my routine is nearly the same every day. I wake up about 6 A.M. to make coffee and get the newspaper off the front lawn. I read each section, starting with sports. The first thing that caught my eye was a picture of Michael on the front page. The article has a title, 'UTA's Michael Choice Projected to be selected in First Round.; After reading the article my adrenaline started flowing. Game on! Nothing could have been better than that. My day was planned. I had to smoke all the meat for approximately 100 invited guests, MLB, UTA, and local news people. Through UTA's Sports Information Director Scott Lacefield, media would be setup in our house, a live feed back to MLB network in New Jersey. What a job he did!

I enjoy smoking meat using pecan wood. The selection of meats included the usual: ribs, chicken, sausage, and brisket. I had never smoked that much meat before. It was a challenge, but I got it done. Although we usually buy everything needed in advance, there are usually odds and ends forgotten the next day. I needed more pecan wood. As I turned down our street returning home, I saw the huge satellite truck with the dish pointed high above, parked in front of our next-door neighbor's house. I was in awe! We had started planning for draft day months ago. The invited guest list grew because Michael has made many friends while attending UTA, and none of them wanted to miss his big day. My wife and her family were used to preparing food for large numbers of people, and several of my wife's friends volunteered to help serve the guests.

Michael seemed to be calm during the morning hours. He stayed busy running errands for his mother. We started receiving guests around 3 P.M. The MLB draft telecast was to start at 6 P.M. CST. I talked with Jeff and Jim, and they were to come to our house later that evening. They had other clients that were draft eligible and needed to be located at the agency office.

The closer we got to 6 P.M., the more people filled our house. There were no available parking spots on our street. I had to tell the neighbors what was going on. When people see a satellite truck, they automatically think a crime has taken place. I promptly made it clear we were hosting a draft party.

At 6 P.M. the MLB Network draft show began. After the panel of analyst was introduced and the stage was set, MLB Commissioner Bud Selig was introduced. He said, "Good evening! Welcome to the 2010 MLB First-Year Player Draft. The Washington Nationals are on the clock."

It's Hard. But It's Fair

The tension was almost unbearable as nine selections had been made. At approximately 7 P.M., Bud Selig said, "With the 10th selection in the first round, the Oakland Athletics select Michael Choice, an outfielder, from the University of Texas at Arlington." All of a sudden, there was a huge roar from the guests in our family room! It was such a huge relief for our family and excitement was everywhere!

The long wait was over! Oakland Athletics selected Michael, and what a relief! The reality that not only was Michael drafted in the first round, but was the 10th pick overall was unbelievable! I started to think about all the outstanding baseball players in America and what an honor for my son to be so fortunate.

Fortunately, we had more than enough food for everyone, including all the media. I received much praise for the smoked meat. I always give the praise to my wife who has the magic touch in seasoning. The pecan wood adds the unmistakable flavor, yet it really is in the seasoning. Once the seasoning marinates in the meat, it's a done deal!

It's Hard. But It's Fair

After everyone left, I sat in the recliner and reflected on the entire day. It was like a storybook. You could not script the draft any better than it played out. There was risk involved, in that no one knows how a draft will fall. The televised portion of the draft covers only the first round (1-32) and supplemental first round (33-49). Fortunately, with Michael being selected No.10, we were happy most of our invited guests were present. We had already said that had he not been selected on the first day of the draft, we would enjoy a planned draft party. Nevertheless, the majority of the area scouts and scouting directors assured Jeff that Michael would definitely get selected in the first round.

Michael was physically exhausted! After rehashing some of the highlights of the day, he fell asleep on the sofa. This was the most exciting day in his life, a dream come true!

Chapter 13
Oakland Athletics Baseball Club

After the June 7 draft, Franklin-Frye Agency went into negotiation with the Oakland A's front office personnel. Jeff Frye moved from our advisor to becoming Michael's agent. As I mentioned earlier, Jeff has a "Jack Russell Terrier" mentality, and I had no doubt he and his staff would negotiate in Michael's best interest. The first thing he asked Michael to do was to be patient. He knew Michael wanted to sign early and get on the field. However, his agency knew from experience that Oakland's initial offer was not acceptable. Franklin-Frye Agency communicated with the A's front office on a weekly basis. The negotiations came to a stall. Jeff told Michael to continue to be patient because only one player taken in the top ten picks had signed a deal. Finally, there were rumors of players drafted after where Michael was taken who reportedly were asking for more than what Michael would sign for. Suddenly negotiations heated up. Michael received a call from Jeff where the A's told him they would give him an answer within 24 hours to Jeff's proposal. Two hours later, Jeff called Michael to say the A's agreed to his offer, and he needed to fly to Arizona to take his physical. Jubilation is what we all felt. Michael was relieved and eager to get back on the baseball field again.

On July 29, 2010, Michael signed a minor league contract, which included a $2 million signing bonus. Armann Brown, the area scout responsible for signing Michael, called our home to congratulate our family on our patience during the negotiations. He had taken my wife and I to dinner shortly after draft day. We were very impressed with his easy, calm demeanor. We really got to know one another well. I believe Armann was able to see we are down to earth, working-class people. My wife was impressed with the bag of Oakland A's logo items he gave our family.

Michael was assigned to the A's rookie league, just so he could get back in baseball shape and get a few at-bats. Eventually the plan was for Michael to travel to Vancouver, Canada, and play for the A's short-season team, the Vancouver Canadians. Once he arrived in Vancouver, he became their everyday center fielder. He gained outstanding experience and helped the Canadians make the playoffs. In less than two full months, Michael put up some respectable numbers, including seven home runs and earning the team's offensive player of the year award.

Michael enjoyed the experience in Vancouver. The players lived with host families. Besides the housing, the families provided meals and transportation to and from the baseball stadium. Michael enjoyed his host family, and they built a warm relationship. Michael became good friends with two of his teammates A.J. Kirby-Jones and Ryan Lipkin. They have visited our home in Grand Prairie, Texas.

It's Hard. But It's Fair

Once the playoff games were over, Michael returned home. After two days of rest, he received a call from Oakland A's asking if he was willing to replace an injured player on the Kane County Cougars, who were in the playoffs in their league. He accepted the invitation. I drove Michael to the airport to catch an early morning flight to Chicago. Later that afternoon, I listened to the radio broadcast as he stepped to the plate in the bottom of the first inning. "It's a deep drive to left center field, home run, Michael Choice!" Incredible! Is what I said out loud. That was very special, and what a way to lift his new team to victory fresh off a 2 ½ hour flight from Dallas Fort Worth. The next day, Michael hit a second home run, but the Cougars came up short. That ended his first professional season. After a couple weeks of rest, he returned to Arizona for instructional training. He and A.J. Kirby-Jones drove to Phoenix together. Instructional training was intense and a huge part of player development. Michael had an opportunity to work one-on-one with MLB Hall of Famer Player Ricky Henderson. Michael told us how special it was to work with a player like Rickey Henderson.

Chapter 14
2011 Oakland Athletics Spring Training Non-Roster Invitee

Michael had an outstanding short season playing for the Vancouver Canadians. He was named "Offensive Player of The Year." The Canadians earned a playoff spot. Unfortunately, they lost two straight games to end their season. After signing his minor league contract on July 29, 2010, Michael played 27 games with the Vancouver Canadians. His overall BA was .284, which included 7 HR's and 26 RBI's. Defensively he had a .968 fielding average. It is fair to say his overall performance was very respectable.

During the winter months, Michael was fortunate to train with Torii Hunter, veteran outfielder with the LA Angels. Besides training, Torii mentored Michael about life as an MLB player. He shared stories he experienced, some not so pleasant, in hopes they would help Michael beware of pitfalls MLB players need to avoid. Torii has played in the league 18 years and has a wealth of experience he used to mentor my son. It is fair to say Michael made a favorable impression on Torii because they worked out together on multiple occasions prior to the start of spring training. It is very admirable when veteran MLB players, like Torii Hunter, take time from their busy schedule to educate young players like Michael. I am certain Michael will do the same one day when he becomes a veteran player. Michael told me how much he appreciated Torii Hunter's generosity.

The Oakland A's extended an invitation to Michael to participate in their 2011 MLB spring training camp as a non-roster invitee. What an honor for

Michael to receive. I knew he would compete on the highest level and articles written confirmed his work on the field turned heads.

Michael was asked to report a week earlier in mid-February, so he could get some additional work in prior to position player's arrival. I agreed to help him drive to Phoenix. It was a seventeen-hour drive, and it was a perfect opportunity for father and son one-on-one communication. Michael is usually not much of a talker, yet on this trip, he was very talkative. He shared many of his experiences from his first year as a professional baseball player. I was all ears and appreciated he was willing to share so very much. I was proud of how he handled the pressure of being a first round draft pick. There are always great expectations an organization has for their top prospects. Michael has always been a hard worker, and his college years at UTA allowed him the opportunity to mature on and off the field. Playing for the 2009 USA Collegiate Baseball Team gave him the experience to play on a big stage.

After the long drive, we arrived in Phoenix totally exhausted. The next morning after a wholesome breakfast, Michael took me to both Oakland A's training facilities. The multiple manicured fields were awesome looking. I could see the huge effort the grounds crew made to get ready for players. I was soaking everything in, knowing my son would prove himself on these fields as he would rise within the Oakland A's organization. Our last stop was to go to the A's main administration building and the stadium where home spring training games were played. I stayed in Michael's truck while he contacted the coaches and management staff. I stared at the lettering on the building, 'Oakland Athletics Baseball Club,' understanding how big a professional baseball club was. For the first time, I realized the two million dollar bonus the A's paid my son was just a small part of how big their franchise was. Michael returned to his truck, and he gave me a thorough tour of Phoenix, including most of the MLB spring training facilities. We were staying in Scottsdale, and I was amazed with the easy access to all your business needs. Nice restaurants were everywhere. I recognized why Phoenix was one of the most desirable cities to live in. Michael was focused on baseball, and I realized me being in Phoenix was a distraction.

The plan was for me to stay in Phoenix three days. After two days, I asked Michael to find me an early morning flight back to Dallas Fort Worth. He needed to devote all his energy to baseball, not baby sit his dad! While flying home, I reflected on what an awesome experience I had with my son. I'll cherish the time he and I had together.

As planned in mid-April, me, my wife Charea, and sister-in-law Freda flew to Phoenix to attend Oakland A's spring training games. What a fabulous time we had. Michael played in seven of the eight games we attended. It was awesome to see him compete on the highest level. In between games, Michael took us to dinner at various restaurants. Our overall spring training experience was better than what we imagined. It gave us a blue print to use while attending future spring training games. Knowing how to navigate to all of the MLB spring training facilities, as well as to identify the most accessible motels are crucial in saving time and money.

There are many twists and turns a professional baseball player must experience while developing the skills good enough to reach the big leagues. Every MLB organization has iconic former players that give of themselves freely by working with top prospects during spring training and fall instructs. The Oakland A's have Hall of Famer Ricky Henderson. Michael was fortunate that Ricky worked one on one with him covering every aspect of the game. After three weeks of training and evaluation, Ricky told Michael, "Listen, you have all the tools to play Major League Baseball right now. Just keep your nose clean and bide your time until you get the call." Michael told me that was the single endorsement he appreciated the most. My mind went back to his college days when I told Michael that one of my favorite all time players was Ricky Henderson, and I was looking for any instructional DVD available on base running by him. He was the best I had ever seen. How ironic that I would do and say those things prior to Michael being drafted by the Oakland A's.

Playing for Oakland A's during 2011 spring training, Michael's stats were very respectable. He played in 15 games with 24 at bats, 7 hits, 8 runs, and .292 batting average. All the veteran players on Oakland's roster did not intimidate Michael. He worked hard and kept his mouth shut. That impressed his teammates, and they respected his work ethic as well. Being able to showcase his skills helped player development define where Michael would be assigned for his first full season of professional baseball.

Charles M. Choice

Chapter 15
Stockton Ports Oakland Athletics Hi-A Affiliate

Michael was assigned to the Stockton Ports in April from the A's spring training camp. The Ports play in the Cal league in Stockton, California. Most of the roster was filled with players who played last year for the Kane County Cougars, A's low A affiliate, and the Vancouver Canadians, A's short season affiliate. The Cal league is known for being hitter friendly because some of the stadiums are configured where the wind blows out the majority of the time. Home runs are hit frequently. However, there are pitcher friendly stadiums as well, where it is extremely hard to hit HR's.

The weather was very hot in Phoenix during spring training with temperatures hovering around 90 degrees. The weather was much colder in Stockton, California in April with temperatures getting no higher than the high 40's. Michael was never a cold weather player. He experienced a very slow start-up to the plate with a batting average around .235. He struck out a lot early on, while his defense was stellar. I really wasn't surprised at all with his slow start because we had seen that before. He would hit much better as the temperature would rise. Michael's first full season would be a grind. With nearly 500 at bats and only a few days off, most players get wore down by seasons end. The long bus trips and required weight lifting and running in between games, as mandated by the strength and conditioning coach, push most players to their limit. Michael never was too fond of weight lifting during the season after he sustained two hairline fractures of his ribs during his freshman year of college. He missed eight games while healing.

June 13th through June 19th, me and my wife Charea flew to California for the Ports home stand against High Desert and Rancho Cucamonga. What a fantastic week we enjoyed. The ports won every game, and Michael was in a zone up to the plate. It was our first opportunity to watch him perform as a professional and an everyday player. We watched outstanding baseball and spent quality time with Michael the entire week. The last game was Father's Day, and Michael did not disappoint. He hit a walk off three run home runs to defeat the Quakes. That was Michael's first walk off home run on any level played. How very proud of him we were that day. Big time players step up when the pressure is the greatest. Down two runs in the bottom of the ninth inning with your parents in the stands identifies maximum pressure. Michael stayed focused and got what he was looking for on that 2 ball, 1 strike pitch, a hanging slider! He hit the ball deep over the left center field fence. We had Father's Day dinner at Red Lobster and flew back home the next morning to Dallas Fort Worth.

The Manager of the Ports Webster Garrison and the hitting coach Brian McArn played very important roles in Michael's baseball progression this past season. A player's development has many ups and downs. How a player deals with failure from one day to the next determines quite a lot. The manager understands his players and is focused on making sure their development is more important than wins and losses. Coach McArn deserves much praise for helping Michael find the right approach as a hitter. Michael put together some excellent numbers offensively. With a few subtle mechanical changes, along with the right consistent approach each at bat, lead to a .285 batting average, 28 doubles, 30 HR's, 82 RBI's, a .376 OBP, and a .542 SLG percentage. Michael told me how much both coaches helped him improve as a player. He cut back on strikeouts the second half of the season with the help of coach McArn.

By July, Michael was on fire as a hitter, raising his batting average more than 35 points. He was named Cal League Player of the Week on 7-11 and Cal League Player of the Month 7-31. The first of August bad luck would occur. While running out an infield hit, Michael strained his left quad. He would miss 13 straight games. Once treatment and rest improved his left leg, Michael got back in the lineup as DH. He played two games and sat out a game. Once the playoffs began, he returned to CF as a starter. Prior to the quad injury, Michael hit 28 HR's. One can only speculate how many long balls he would hit had the injury not occurred. Yet injuries are a part of the game, and you have to live with the interruption.

The Stockton Ports earned a playoff berth and won the best of three games in the first round against the Modesto Nuts. With that accomplishment, they faced the San Jose Giants in the best of five games for the Cal League North Division Championship. They won in four games. The Ports lost the Cal League Championship in four games to the Lake Elsinore Storm. Michael had outstanding playoff games, leading all hitters with a .426 batting average, including 3 HR's, and three doubles, and 10 RBI's.

With the season over, Michael received the following additional honors. The Stockton Ports named Michael 2011 Player of the Year. He was selected to Cal League Post All-Star Team on 8-31. Baseball America named Michael first team Outfield, Hi-A level, Minor League Baseball on 9-16.

With the completion of his first full year of professional baseball, it is fair to say Michael had a stellar season. Much has been said about the Cal league being a hitter friendly league, but in reality, there were a few ballparks that were pitcher friendly as well. Michael hit Thirty HR's, a feat not many ball players can accomplish in a season on any professional level.

The Oakland A's selected Michael to play in the Arizona Fall League for the Phoenix Desert Dogs. This was an opportunity for Michael to play against many of the top prospects in professional baseball. Michael played in 17 games, with 66 AB, 21 hits, 5 2B, 6 HR, 18 RBI, .423 OBP, and .667 SLG.

Near the end of the Arizona Fall League season, Michael was selected to play in the "Rising Stars Game," 25 players each representing the Eastern Division and Western Division. He went one for three, including a walk and run scored helping the Western Division beat the Eastern Division 11 to 2. The game was televised nationally on the MLB network. His outstanding overall play will inch him closer to his ultimate goal of making it to the big leagues.

Charles M. Choice

Chapter 16
Midland RockHounds
Oakland Athletics Double AA Affiliate

Oakland A's double AA affiliate is the Midland RockHounds of the Texas League. What a huge difference from playing in Stockton, California. Midland, Texas is located in west Texas, known for constant strong winds. Sand storms were the normal for most of the home games. Balls hit to the outfield were often affected by strong winds. I have seen balls hit to high left field pushed to right field or to right field bleachers. Sand storms during day games affected the outcome of most games played. The RockHounds usually had a distinct advantage against visiting teams. Outfield play was crucial, and setting your defense to combat the strong winds was a necessity in winning games. It is safe to say no one enjoyed playing games in Midland. Most RockHound players wanted to serve their time in Midland and then move on. Michael played well in Midland after a stellar season playing for the Stockton Ports in 2011, where he was selected as co-organizational player of the year.

As usual, Michael started out slow, adjusting to the cold temperatures and strong gusting winds in Midland, Texas. Outfield play made most players look ridiculous from one game to another. The coaches understood this and encouraged their players to make adjustments by moving players throughout the game as wind gusts fluctuated most of the time. Generally the wind blew in making homeruns nearly impossible. Michael hit a lot of line shots in the gaps that usually stayed below the gusting winds.

Pitching was much tougher in AA. As a hitter, adjustments had to be made as scouting reports on hitters and pitchers was readily available. Pitchers had command of multiple pitches with various speeds. Hitter's weaknesses were exploited. To be successful on this level, the mental aspect of the game determines who finds success. Reviewing game tapes help players understand what adjustments to make to become better hitters. Michael worked hard and improved in all aspects of the game. In late July, Michael was hit by a pitch on his left hand, causing a fracture to his left hand. His season ended abruptly after being red hot as a hitter. His year-end statistics were: Games played 91, At Bats 359, Runs Scored 59, Hits 103, Total Bases 152, 2B 15, 3B 2, BB 33, HR 10, RBI 58, Batting Average .287. Michael's stats for the season were very respectable for a shortened season. Michael was almost assured to be promoted to Oakland A's affiliate triple AAA Sacramento River Cats next season.

For Michael's season to end so abruptly was very disappointing for our family, considering how hot a hitter he was at the time. For our family, it was very tough to digest. We went through baseball withdraws with no more games for Michael to play in 2012. Michael seemed to accept his fate and returned home to heal his fractured hand. Seeing the huge cast on his left arm was a reminder how fragile staying healthy really was. Regardless to how talented you are, careers can end in an instance. We appreciate every game Michael has played.

My wife and I enjoyed the relatively short drive to Midland from the Dallas area to watch games. There wasn't much to offer in Midland besides professional baseball. The stadium was very nice with good food and entertainment. Rocky the mascot was very active and had a swagger he showed at every game. We enjoyed several weekend series during the season. Many staff members recognized us as Michael's parents, threating us very well. These were favorable experiences we appreciated.

Chapter 17
Sacramento River Cats
AAA Affiliate of The Oakland Athletics

In the spring of 2013, Michael was promoted to the Sacramento River Cats of the Pacific Coast League. After a successful spring training as a non-roster invitee, Michael began perhaps his best overall year in the minor leagues. Many scouts will tell you that the pitching in AAA is a real test for top prospects. Many pitchers on this level have had some MLB experience.

From the beginning of the season and throughout, Michael played well and provided strong offensive results from the middle of the batting order. He hit for power and average as a run producer. Defensively he played centerfield with outstanding skills and above average outfield assist numbers.

His final statistics for the 2013 were as follows. Games played 132, AB 510, runs 90, hits 154, total bases 227, 2B 29, 3B 1, HR 14, RBI 89, BB 69, batting average .302. Michael was selected to the post season Pacific Coast League All Star Team.

Michael has played at every minor league level. His overall skill level has improved each year. We watched all of his games on the computer. This was the first year we were unable to watch any of his games live. With the difference in time zones, we often stayed up after midnight watching complete games. As parents, we have accepted what was available, enjoying every moment.

The Oakland Athletics have developed Michael the right way, and I am confident he was ready to join the show. His work ethic and positive results speak clearly.

Chapter 18
Oakland Athletics Baseball Club

On September 01, 2013, Michael was promoted to the Oakland Athletics Baseball Club. It was the ultimate achievement for Michael. Our family was astatic with joy! Michael called us around midnight with the good news. He told us to prepare to fly to Oakland later that morning. He made our flight arrangements and like a dream, we arrived in Oakland in the early afternoon. We got to the stadium just in time to see his 1st at bat for his MLB debut 09-02-2013. We were blessed to be in Oakland to celebrate with Michael after achieving his ultimate goal of reaching the major leagues. Witnessing his 1st MLB hit off Texas Ranger pitcher Martin Perez was a very special moment we will always remember. After many minor league games, long bus rides, his dream had finally become reality. Many players toil for years in the minor leagues, never getting promoted to MLB. He will always remember this day for a lifetime. The Oakland Athletics authenticated the baseball and bat of his 1st hit, now sitting in his trophy case.

Michael's overall stats in September were respectable. Games played 9, At Bats 18, Runs 2, Hits 5, Total Bases 6, 2B 1, BB 1, batting Average .278.

Attending games in Oakland Alameda Coliseum was an awesome experience! The fans are loud and very different. Loud music playing was non -stop. Low attendance was the norm, yet excitement was electric! Everywhere.

On December 3rd, Michael was traded to the Texas Rangers. It was my birthday, and we all were caught off guard. I was shopping at Forever Young Records in Grand Prairie, Texas when I received a phone call from Michael, asking why I wasn't answering my cell phone. He went on to tell me about the trade. I was filled with excitement realizing Michael would be returning home to play for the team he grew up loving. Rarely does a player get an opportunity to play for a team in his back yard. We had a nice celebration at Michael's house with family and close friends.

Chapter 19
Texas Rangers Baseball Club

The month of December was quite eventful. We were filled with excitement daily with the many newspaper articles welcoming Michael back to Arlington to play baseball in his hometown after a stellar collegiate baseball career at UTA. General Manager Jon Daniels held a news conference with the media, saying that left field was Michael Choice's to win. As a family, we were living a dream. For Michael, it was the fact he could sleep in his own bed with a 20-minute drive from his house to Globe Life Park Stadium.

Then two weeks later, the Texas Rangers dropped a bomb by signing free agent Shin-Soo Choo to a $110 million ten year contract to play left field. All of a sudden, all the air came rushing out of our family balloon. There was some real disappointment with the Rangers latest transaction. However, Michael refocused to getting ready for spring training by being in the best physical condition possible. He was setting the goal of earning a spot on the 25-man roster.

Manager Ron Washington called Michael into his spring training office in Surprise, Arizona and told him, "Just be yourself, not any other player, that being Michael Choice would be good enough for him." Michael followed the skipper's advice and had an outstanding spring training, leading all hitters in batting average, earning himself an opening day roster spot. He earned respect from his teammates and coaching staff. We were both proud and extremely happy for him. Hard work had definitely paid off. Opening day was a spectacular event. We sat in the Ranger family section and witnessed the introduction of all players and coaches. Hearing Michael being introduced to the sellout crowd was a moment we will always treasure.

On April 12, 2014, with the Rangers down 5-4 in the bottom of the 9th against the Houston Astros, Manager Ron Washington called on Michael to pinch hit. He did not disappoint as he hit his 1st MLB home run 407 ft. to centerfield to tie the game off LH pitcher Kevin Chapman in front of 45,000 loud Ranger fans, including my wife and me. What an awesome experience that was. The roar from the fans was beyond my imagination, a moment that will be etched in our mines for a lifetime. That was the biggest baseball moment in Michael's baseball career. As he stepped on home plate, he pointed to the sky, giving thanks to the Lord above and to both grandmothers, Amanda and Betty Jo, watching from heaven.

Michael would hit eight more home runs that year off some very good pitchers, including Cy Young winner, Justin Verlander. His stats overall were respectable for a rookie, games played 43, AB 253, R 20, H 43, TB 81, 2B 6, 3B 1, HR 9, RBI 36, BB 21, Batting Ave .182. Most MLB rookies struggle their first year, but 9 HR's and 36 RBI was not bad by my opinion.

Near the end of the 2014 season, Manager Ron Washington abruptly resigned for personal reasons to the shock of everyone. Bench coach Tim Bogart was chosen as the interim Manager and did an outstanding job, as the players responded well to his leadership. Michael played well and continued to hit with power. Against the visiting Atlanta Braves, Michael hit a triple and a double his 1st two at bats. His 3rd at bat, Michael hit a deep drive to the left centerfield gap that looked like another triple. As he approached 2nd base, he grabbed his left hamstring. He had to be helped off the field ending his 2014 season. An MRI exam the following day revealed a hamstring tear.

The Texas Rangers snubbed Tim Bogart and hired Jeff Banister manager, former assistant coach with the Pittsburg Pirates, to the shock of almost everyone. Tim Bogart had taken over for Ron Washington with a very respectful winning streak to end the 2014 season. That seemed to ensure he would be signed as permanent Manager for the Rangers organization in 2015. Jon Daniels decided differently, by hiring Jeff Banister.

Michael gave me a wonderful Father's Day gift in June, flying me to Seattle to watch the Rangers play the Mariners weekend series. I stayed at the same hotel as the Rangers. What an awesome trip for me. Michael and I had lunch Saturday at one of the local restaurants. When we walked into our hotel, I noticed Ron Washington sitting in the lobby. Michael asked me if I would like

It's Hard. But It's Fair

to meet him. I said of course. That was a special moment for me. I told the Skipper I was happy my son had the opportunity to play for him.

Michael Choice was clearly a Ron Washington player and Tim Bogart's as well. It would be clear in early 2015 spring training that Michael would not fit in the Texas Rangers future plans. Michael got only 15 AB's and was sent down to AAA Round Rock Express. Once again, I saw the business side of MLB. Players are moved around like pawns in a chess game until the teams lose control and players achieve free agency.

Michael's professional baseball career continues, as the Texas Rangers traded him to the Cleveland Indians August 21, 2015. Stay tuned!

Chapter 20
In Conclusion

Michael feels his professional baseball career so far has been very rewarding. All the years I coached, Michael I'd say the same words over and over, "**It's Hard**. But **It's Fair**" Among several tattoos, Michael has those words scripted on his left bicep. When I played college football in Georgia, our head football coach, the late L.S. Epps, belted those same words during the two-a-day practices in late August, where the sweltering heat and humidity in Georgia was almost unbearable. Players were pushed to the very edge while completing the many drills and live scrimmages. What coach Epps was trying to convey to his players with those words was the road to success is difficult, requiring the most dedicated work ethic and perseverance. To achieve greatness athletically, you will be rewarded with how much you put into it. I was very surprised when Michael showed me that tattoo. It was an affirmation that those words had motivated him over the years to stay focused on working to be the very best he could be! He also wrote, "**Living The Dream**" under the bill of his UTA ball cap for three consecutive years, expressing his love of the game.

    I have pointed out in this book the decline of African American youth playing baseball in America. There have been significant national efforts by several groups to improve the percentages of African Americans playing in MLB. In the early nineties, participation was approximately 8.5%, dropping to 5% in 2011. One of the programs making the strongest efforts to improve the numbers is Reviving Baseball in the Inner Cities (RBI). This program was started by John Young, former MLB player and scout in 1989 for boys in south central Los Angeles, motivating considerable numbers of African American youth to sign up and play baseball. In 1991, Major League Baseball began administrating the (RBI) program and has provided more than $30,000,000.00 in resources, in cooperation with major sporting goods companies, and others. The (RBI) program has grown to over 200 cities internationally. It is very likely we will see the number of African Americans playing in MLB to grow significantly in the years to come.

Because of the large number of Latin players in MLB, it is understandable why the general public is unaware of dwindling numbers of African Americans playing. Most see skin color and never look any closer that there may be a problem. In most Latin countries, baseball is very popular where children start playing at an early age. In African American communities, parents often wait until it is too late to encourage their children to play baseball. Most children attempting to play baseball at age eleven or twelve find they are too far behind to compete with others that have been playing since the age of five. The other consideration within the African American community is basketball and football are more popular. The high cost of playing baseball is another valid reason given for the declining participation, yet it is my opinion the lack of popularity is the more significant of the two.

Nevertheless, there are African American baseball players like Michael Choice who have played baseball from an early age that have been overlooked by college recruiters and professional scouts. Many have chosen to follow the well-established high school baseball programs that often don't have any African Americans on their teams. If they simply followed the top performers statistically in the area, then the Michael Choice's would be found. My hope is that his baseball story will motivate parents to encourage their children to play baseball. Hopefully my book helps parents by offering the points I've made for their consideration, prior to them making crucial decisions that could benefit their children. Keep in mind, Michael Choice was like many other children in America. He fell in love with baseball at an early age and has taken us on a marvelous journey we have enjoyed all the way!

There is no easy path to the major leagues, yet with a strong work ethic and a tremendous desire within, it's a real possibility! The most important advice we have given Michael is, "Always give the good Lord above all the praise for blessing him with the talent to play this great game of baseball, and everything will work out for the best!"

Michael Choice
Texas Rangers

Charles Michael Choice
Author